University of
Chester

Other titles in the series

CILT, the National Centre for Languages, seeks to support and develop multilingualism and intercultural competence among all sectors of the population in the UK.

CILT serves education, business and the wider community with:
- specialised and impartial information services;
- high quality advice and professional development;
- expert support for innovation and development;
- quality improvement in language skills and service provision.

CILT is a charitable trust, supported by the DfES and other Government departments throughout the UK.

NEW PATHFINDER

Raising the standard

Addressing the needs of gifted and talented pupils

1

ANNELI MCLACHLAN

The author and publisher would like to thank copyright holders for the permission granted to reproduce copyright material, as detailed next to the relevant excerpts.

First published 2002
by the Centre for Information on Language Teaching and Research (CILT)
20 Bedfordbury
London
WC2N 4LB

Copyright © Centre for Information on Language Teaching and Research 2002

ISBN 1 902031 96 2

A catalogue record for this book is available from the British Library

Printed in Great Britain by Hobbs the Printers Ltd, Totton, Hampshire

CILT Publications are available from: Central Books, 99 Wallis Rd, London E9 5LN. Tel: 0845 458 9910. Fax: 0845 458 9912. Book trade representation (UK and Ireland): Broadcast Book Services, Charter House, 27a London Road, Croydon CR0 2RE. Tel: 020 8681 8949. Fax: 020 8688 0615.

contents

Acknowledgements

I would like to thank Heinemann, Harper Collins, Folens and Accelerated Learning Systems for permission to reproduce their materials in this book. I would also like to thank Dave Baker, John Broadbent, Victor Burgess, David Buckland, Colin Christie, Alan Dobson, Kate Green, Simon Green, Vee Harris, Alex Harvey, Bernardette Holmes, Jeff Lee, Hillary Lowe, Siân Maddrell, Eleanor Mayes, Iain Mitchell, Rosanna Raimato, Leanda Reed, Glenis Shaw, Dick Smith, Françoise Vidal and Marcus Waltl for their invaluable input. I would also like to thank teachers I met in Barking and Dagenham, Greenwich, Harrow, and Waltham Forest for their ideas and enthusiasm. Finally, thanks to pupils in masterclasses from Elliott School, Sheringdale, Brandlehow, Allfarthing, Honeywell, Granard and Hotham primary schools in Wandsworth for the privilege of teaching you.

Introduction

Raising the standard: addressing the needs of gifted and talented pupils considers how we can motivate high ability pupils at all levels, from Key Stage 2 through GCSE to advanced level study, to achieve to the best of their ability. It aims to show how we can successfully tap the potential of able learners – some of whom may be underachieving – whilst considering how our approach to gifted and talented pupils can benefit our teaching of **all** pupils. The government has focused our attention on this issue now, with its Excellence in Cities initiative. As language teachers, we are thus able to put our methodology for teaching our most able under scrutiny in order to establish best practice.

Excellence in Cities – gifted and talented children

The national strategy for the education of gifted and talented children forms one of the seven main policy strands of the Excellence in Cities initiative. Excellence in Cities focused initially on six large conurbations – Inner London, Birmingham, Manchester/Salford, Liverpool/Knowsley, Leeds/Bradford and Sheffield/Rotherham. It consists of a three-year action programme with year one designated a pilot year. The programme has given rise to much good practice in languages, which merits dissemination. In Chapter 5 we consider the summer schools and masterclasses arising from the initiative. Excellence in Cities provides a lever for raising standards not only for the 5–10% of pupils for whom a 'distinct teaching and learning programme' is put in place, but also for other pupils who benefit from a close examination of teaching and learning styles. In short, whilst focusing on the most able, the initiative has begun to drive up standards for all. *Raising the standard* aims to give practical examples of how this is happening in Modern Foreign Languages.

Following Excellence in Cities, Excellence Clusters are being developed to bring Excellence in Cities to smaller areas of deprivation, including coastal towns, deprived rural areas, ex-coalfield and industrial towns. The need to examine methodology in the light of the initiative is thus a national priority.

What does this mean for languages?

The requirement to provide a 'distinct teaching and learning programme' for our most able 5–10% of pupils spurs us on to consider our practice in general. As language teachers, we need to examine what we ask our pupils to do in and out of the classroom on a regular basis. We are required to analyse what we expect our pupils to achieve and to ask ourselves if our expectations are appropriate for our most able learners. Do gifted and talented pupils enjoy languages? How can we help them to flourish? We are offered an exciting context and an opportunity to improve pupils' learning experience. The challenge in language teaching is **how** to do this. Does our everyday teaching **engage** our most able pupils? Do we differentiate to meet their needs effectively? How can we improve our current offer? Is there scope for extra-curricular activities? These are the questions that this book sets out to address.

We need, therefore, to establish who our gifted and talented pupils are, how we can identify them and how we then communicate with our identified pupils (Chapter 1). Within this context, it will be important to consider how gifted and talented pupils are treated. Should they be made to feel special? Does special treatment of the gifted and talented lead to resentment on the part of our other pupils? How should we group our pupils? What are the social implications of our groupings?

Whilst catering for our gifted and talented pupils affords us the opportunity to reflect and then to innovate, it also poses difficult questions about how the issue is to be handled at a school and a departmental level. Such questions need to be discussed openly.

We need to consider what type of tasks more able pupils should be doing and in which contexts (Chapters 2 and 4). Such questions afford us the opportunity to examine the diet we offer to all pupils and to address the problem of poor motivation amongst language learners. Such an analysis is timely within the context of a revised National Curriculum and revised GCSE specifications, which herald a welcome shift back to:

- knowledge about language;
- a practical knowledge and understanding of language structures and grammar;
- developing language skills and language learning skills;
- cultural awareness.

This constitutes a move away from the drive to accumulate language within numerous topic areas, which is perhaps perpetuated by some coursebooks, and which, as we will see in Chapter 2, can be a turn-off not just for our most able, but for all pupils.

Do our pupils do enough of the work? Do we do all the teaching, while they are not undertaking enough of the learning? In Chapter 3, *Raising the standard* will consider how we can increase the range of teaching and learning styles. Gifted and talented pupils often have preferred learning styles and are thus able to bring benefits for all. I will focus on the importance of teaching learners how to learn and look at the practicalities of this process.

We can offer our gifted and talented children access to learning opportunities beyond the classroom and the conventional school day. Chapter 5 will consider extension and enrichment opportunities, along with the effective use of ICT as a means of expanding pupils' skills. This chapter will also look at the practicalities of fast-tracking and acceleration, and will introduce the new AEAs – advanced extension awards, which give able pupils an opportunity to demonstrate a greater depth of understanding, whilst testing their ability to think critically and respond creatively to a range of challenging tasks at A grade level in advanced level study.

The case study will focus on accelerated learning in French and Italian at The Grey Coat Hospital School in London.

Raising the standard aims to show, by dint of practical examples, how gifted and talented pupils provide another facet of the many differences within our schools and thus enable us to celebrate the diversity of which our educational establishments are justly proud.

Throughout this book the terms 'gifted and talented', 'able' and 'more able' will be used to describe our target pupils.

Defining
able learners

- [ ] How do I spot them?

- [ ] Will they be good at all subjects?

- [ ] Will they be strong in all skills?

- [ ] Are bilingual pupils naturally gifted and talented?

- [ ] What do I do when I've identified someone as gifted and talented?

- [ ] Should I make gifted and talented pupils feel special?

- [ ] Will they get above themselves?

chapter 1

How do I spot them?

Research has been undertaken on identifying gifted and talented pupils across the curriculum. Many of the general characteristics identified also apply to language learners. For example pupils may have 'exceptional curiosity and want to know why' (Wallace). They may 'have a preference for the company of older children and adults' (Leyden). They may 'possess superior powers of reasoning, of dealing with abstractions, of generalising from specific facts, of understanding meanings and seeing into relationships' (Laycock). These are, without question, characteristics that are discernible in language learners and in language lessons. In Chapter 2, we will consider how to meet the learning needs of able language learners, but we must first define our subject specific identification criteria. The following list is broad, but not exhaustive. Indeed, it is important that identification criteria are established within one's own school context, where different conditions may prevail. Appendix 2 provides a less theoretical checklist of what to look out for when identifying gifted and talented pupils.

Within a Modern Foreign Languages (MFL) context, gifted and talented pupils are likely to:

• have a strong desire to put language together by themselves;

> *... they apply principles from what they have learned to new situations, transforming phrases and using them in a different context, often with humour ... ('Guidance on teaching gifted and talented pupils',* QCA (**www.nc.uk.net/gt**))

Gifted and talented pupils can see how language operates. They can infer grammatical patterns and will invent systems for themselves. They push the boundaries of language learning and want to transfer their knowledge to different contexts. They want to play with language to amuse themselves and others. It is important that we acknowledge and encourage such creativity.

• show creativity and imagination when using language;

> *... they extend the boundaries of their knowledge and work beyond what they have learned, not wishing simply to respond and imitate, but to initiate exchanges and to create new language ...* (ibid)

Gifted and talented pupils find constant repetition of the same type of task, or practice of skills with which they are already familiar, a turn-off. They are not content simply to 'parrot'. How many times do we ask them to do this in the language classroom? Perhaps too many ... Chapter 2 will consider the nature of higher order tasks which might engage more able pupils more successfully. One of the solutions adopted by these pupils in order to make things more interesting is the desire to create new language. The invention of able pupils can lead to some rewarding teaching moments and can be of immense benefit to their classmates (who are being shown the way to some extent), who are seeing learning strategies first-hand and witnessing the possibilities of creativity.

• have a natural feel for language;

> *... they are willing to take risks and see what works, knowing instinctively what sounds right, and what looks right; they are acutely and swiftly aware of the relationship between sound and spelling ...*
> (ibid)

We need to create an environment and set up tasks where pupils are encouraged to take those risks in learning and experimenting. Able pupils when pressed often say 'It just looks right' or 'That doesn't sound right'. One of our aims should be to enable them to analyse these instinctive reactions and to give them the metalanguage to be able to express this.

As an alternative to being swiftly aware of the sound–spelling relationship, more able pupils may develop their own phonetic systems and may need to be reminded of the importance of correct orthography. This can lead to interesting discussions in class.

• pick up new language and structures quickly;

> *... they may have excellent aural and oral skills and may be able to cope with rapid streams of sound and identify key words at an early stage; they may also display outstanding powers of retention, both immediately and from one lesson to the next ...* (ibid)

Listening is a notoriously difficult skill. Able pupils are often able to shine in this skill, confounding teachers' expectations. We need to plan accordingly and consider the nature of the tasks that we are demanding of these pupils. The power to absorb and reproduce vocabulary and structures from one lesson to the next can also be remarkably exciting. In Chapter 5 we will consider how this can be used to the teacher's advantage.

• make connections and classify words and structures to help them learn more efficiently;

> *... they are able to evaluate new language critically, recognising the grammatical function of words ...* (ibid)

The National Literacy Strategy has helped all pupils enormously with regard to grammatical definitions and powers of analysis and will have been of particular interest to gifted and talented pupils, given that linguistic manipulation is a spur for able language learners. It allows them scope for problem-solving. It also allows them to apply their own systems, to generate and create. Grammar allows them to look at patterns and to apply them in different contexts. It also reduces the need for repetition and for reliance on non-verbal support. All these factors combine to make grammar an area of interest for able language learners. We will consider the role of grammar and how we might approach it in Chapter 4.

• seek solutions and ask further questions;

> *... they may test out their theories and seek to solve linguistic problems, sometimes challenging the tasks set, and trying to understand their relevance to the language-learning process ...* (ibid)

Able pupils want to know **why**. They may well question the relevance of a task they are being required to complete if they feel they have mastered a number of vocabulary items or a particular grammatical structure, and that they are being required to perform a repetitive task. Teacher response here is key. Teacher awareness of the tasks and activities we set up within the classroom can lead to improved motivation and performance on the part of all pupils.

Able pupils may have a 'devastating appreciation of the weaknesses of other people including those in positions of authority such as teachers' (Teare). This is not what tired teachers want to experience at the end of a six-period day! It is therefore important that we include in our planning the need for able pupils to be given a broader context within which to operate, including higher order tasks such as those which require pupils to compare and contrast, to generalise and hypothesise, rather than simply answering content-driven questions on a text, for example. MFL is a subject that is extremely well placed to challenge able pupils. We must meet that challenge.

- have an insight into their own learning style and preference;

> *... they may say how they like to learn vocabulary or structures; they are clear about the types of task they like doing, they may show or display an ability to work independently, without supervision, and to make effective use of reference material ...* (ibid)

I will discuss this issue further in Chapter 4. Able learners can be very useful within the classroom context from this point of view. They can provide a model for teachers to hold up as an example to others. They can show how success is achieved. Their insight into their own learning style is often the key to their success and can help others on the way. We need to improve their skills repertoire, however, and not just allow them to adopt the learning strategy which they find comes easiest to them. We can show them different ways of working and challenge their approaches. This type of teaching pays dividends not just for the 5–10% most able pupils, but for all our charges.

- show an intense interest in cultural features of the language being studied;

> *... they may use idiom in the language itself and explore the history and the traditions of the language; some pupils may wish to share their knowledge with their peers ...* (ibid)

Language learning perhaps focuses too narrowly on the language itself and often on transactional tasks. Sadly, given the demands of the National Curriculum and the GCSE, teachers may feel that there is little time to introduce pupils properly to the culture of the countries where the language is being spoken. For all our pupils' sake, we should re-examine our approach to culture, to the way young people live their lives in the countries where the target language is spoken, to traditions, food, music, television soap operas, history, geography, politics, making the language of such integral to our teaching. Able pupils provide us with an incentive to dwell on such aspects of culture. They often become particularly interested in issues specific to countries. They will bring things into the classroom. We will look at how to exploit this enthusiasm in Chapter 3.

As well as broadening the cultural outlook, we can look at different models of teaching and different ways of working, such as Content and Language Integrated Learning (CLIL) and bilingual sections already in existence – this will be examined further in Chapter 5.

Will they be good at all subjects?

It is important to make a distinction between pupils who are able across the board and the gifted and talented cohort. Finely tuned identification criteria like those outlined above should do the job for us. There may, of course, amongst the pupils identified, be some who figure across all subject areas. School co-ordinators will concern themselves with further provision for all-rounders, while making sure that practitioners share observations and communicate with each other in order to employ the most successful approaches for particular individuals. If we are applying our subject-specific criteria correctly, then it matters little if names appear in other subject areas. However, it is often the case that MFL throws up some surprises in the identification exercise. This is perhaps due to the nature of what are often orally-based lessons. Excellence in Cities, as an initiative, is keen to tackle underachievement, to identify pupils who have potential, but who – for whatever reason – are not fulfilling it at present. Many schools, therefore, also monitor their cohorts to make sure that there is appropriate representation of gender, class and ethnic community, and regularly review the names that figure on the list.

Will they be strong in all skills?

As mentioned above, some gifted and talented pupils are all-rounders across the curriculum, while others may show a gift or a talent for one particular subject. Similarly, some pupils may display a well-developed aural or oral facility, while others may prefer to read and write. Those pupils who prefer grammatical accuracy and the written word – many gifted and talented pupils prefer to work on their own – may shy away from oral work and have real difficulty with pronunciation. But their written work may be almost 100% accurate! It is possible to be more gifted and talented in one skill than another and individual departmental guidelines should be designed to offer help to teachers here. I would argue very strongly for looking at skills individually. We can thus identify pupils with potential and tailor their programme to enable them to improve in other skill areas.

Are bilingual pupils naturally gifted and talented?

Bilingual pupils may have lived in another country or may speak another language at home. Bilingual pupils bring a wealth of diversity and knowledge to the language classroom, but the pupils themselves may not be gifted and talented in MFL.

Bilingual pupils often have well-developed oral fluency, but may not have such a firm grasp of the written form of the language they speak. Bilingual pupils will need an individualised course of study if they are to fulfil their potential.

If they are bilingual in a language which is on offer at the school, they might follow an individualised programme in their own language, allowing them to sit exams early, to follow an extended reading programme, to exploit ICT possibilities, and to have time with the Foreign Language Assistant (FLA), while studying a second MFL on timetable.

What do I do when I've identified someone as gifted and talented?

This depends largely on school policy, where a 'distinct teaching and learning programme' should have been established and where provision may be made for out-of-school activities. Schools may also consider acceleration or fast-tracking (see Chapter 5).

Some departments arrange for withdrawal periods for more able pupils. It may be possible for departments to organise pupils to work either as individuals or in small groups away from their teaching group but still under departmental supervision. Whenever possible, pupils of like ability should be given the opportunity to work together. Other departments prefer to see the more able pupil as part of the class and a potential resource. Withdrawal is not necessarily their preferred way of bringing these pupils on.

More able pupils may require access to extra materials and/or equipment to maximise their development. Funds are obviously required here. Departments can make gifted and talented pupils a regular agenda item. Such an approach stimulates debate as to appropriate methodology for able pupils and often gives rise to fruitful discussion.

Departments might also consider appointing mentors to their pupils – a key member of staff or a more senior pupil, who will provide subject specific guidance.

Should I make gifted and talented pupils feel special?

This is a very difficult question indeed. All children are special and should be made to feel special. It may be school policy to tell pupils and parents who the gifted and talented cohort are and then to involve them in enrichment and enhancement activities. Obviously, pupils need to know who they are if they are to be involved in out-of-school activities. Some schools do not exclude *any* pupils from enrichment activities, however, targeting the gifted and talented cohort first and foremost and then inviting all other pupils or suggesting that each member of the cohort 'bring a friend'. Individual school situations therefore frequently determine policy.

It may be departmental policy to monitor gifted and talented pupils discreetly in order to ensure appropriate differentiation and progress. Public identification, if not handled sensitively, can lead to resentment and stigmatisation. It is important, therefore, that there is a debate on this question both at school policy level and at departmental policy level.

For me, the ideal situation would be to have the gifted and talented initiative working within a school ethos where difference and diversity is viewed positively. At Elliott School in Putney, the opening paragraph of the policy on gifted and talented pupils reads:

> *Elliott is a comprehensive school which sets out to provide an inclusive education for students of all cultures, genders and social classes. It aims to provide the most suitable educational opportunity possible for each individual pupil. To do so entails the identification of the most able, and provision of suitable experiences and teaching programmes to enrich and enhance them, so that they are able to meet to the fullest possible extent their personal potential.*

The focus therefore is on meeting the needs of the individual.

Will they get above themselves?

The social dimension of having a gifted and talented policy is not to be underestimated. Whilst teachers recognise that enhancement is important and that a close examination of the tasks that we set can benefit all pupils, the implementation of a successful policy requires sensitive handling amongst children.

> *'Why is she always getting special treatment?'*

> *'I want to do what he's doing.'*

> *'Why doesn't Johnny have to do the first exercise, Miss?'*

Such questions can arise if the basic premise is not addressed, namely that, in line with the principles of comprehensive education, all pupils have different needs and these needs must be met. This is an issue of equal opportunities. Teachers might wish to say at various junctures: 'Alex has different needs. We are all different.'

Withdrawal of pupils also needs to be treated with sensitivity, particularly if more able pupils are working with FLAs. This can be viewed as a privilege denied to others and, as such, needs to be carefully thought through.

Materials for departments

The following materials might provide a focus for in service training via departmental discussion or perhaps comparison with what is already in place in your school.

A sample departmental policy: gifted and talented pupils

Pupils of marked ability are identified in accordance with school policy, and their needs are defined. Provision for native speakers is the responsibility of the head of department, who will assess the level of competence and suggest appropriate materials/tuition, perhaps involving the FLAs.

Criteria for identifying gifted and talented pupils in languages

Pupils displaying marked ability in languages will be highly competent in all four skill areas, although one area may be particularly strong. More specifically, a pupil will display some of the following characteristics:

- He or she has excellent powers of retention and recall.
- He or she has well developed aural discrimination skills.
- He or she possesses the capacity to generate language with ease, and often orally and in writing.
- He or she demonstrates an awareness of idiom.
- He or she can transfer knowledge readily from a familiar to an unfamiliar context.
- He or she demonstrates an awareness of register.
- He or she possesses and exploits an extended vocabulary.
- He or she is eager to expand his or her repertoire.

Provision/support for gifted and talented pupils

Enhancement – teachers will ensure that challenging work is provided for these pupils, both in class and at home. Such tasks may be based on the texts undertaken by other pupils, differing in the task set, but may also be distinct. Pupils will be encouraged to exercise independence in their learning and will be expected to use reference materials and to research within work with a degree of autonomy.

Acceleration – the head of department will decide if a gifted and talented pupil is to be entered early for examinations. Such a decision will only be made if there is suitable provision for extension of the pupil after he or she has taken the exam.

Withdrawal – pupils may, at times, be withdrawn to work with the FLAs or with cross-age tutors in order to improve their performance.

Access to materials/equipment – the department seeks to provide materials which challenge the pupil. These may include more complex textbooks, extended reading practice, grammar practice, working with ICT.

Mentoring – a member of the department will act as mentor to those pupils nominated as being gifted and talented. The list of these pupils will be reviewed termly. The mentor will liaise with the Gifted and Talented Co-ordinator in his or her support of pupils.

Monitoring one's policy

How successful is your policy for developing gifted and talented pupils?

1. Do you have ways in which gifted and talented pupils are identified and monitored from an early stage?

2. Are all sectors of the school community able to reach the highest levels of achievement?

3 Do you have a broad, balanced curriculum for gifted and talented pupils as well as for the group as a whole?

   For example:
   - skills;
   - materials;
   - ICT;
   - contact with native speakers.

4. Are gifted and talented pupils challenged sufficiently to develop their skills, knowledge and understanding and are they given opportunities to apply their skills, knowledge and understanding in a variety of contexts?

5. Can gifted and talented pupils evaluate their own work critically, identify their strengths and weaknesses and improve their own learning?

6. Does your use of oral work encourage real thinking and learning rather than just recall?

7. Do parents understand and know how best to support the work that their child is doing in MFL at home and at school?

8. How do parents, colleagues, other pupils respond to the work of individuals and the whole group? Is work valued appropriately?

9. Are there opportunities for displaying work, for holding exhibitions and for involving individuals and groups in the process?

10. Do you maintain records of the achievements of the most able pupils year on year?

11. Are you aware of the performance of individuals in other areas of the curriculum?

12. What happens to pupils when they move on in the school? To other schools? Beyond school?

key points	• Criteria for identification of gifted and talented pupils are available at www.nc.uk.net.gt
	• Departments need to establish a coherent approach to the gifted and talented cohort
	• Teachers have an obligation to meet the needs of gifted and talented pupils

Coping with the challenge of able learners

- [ ] Gifted and talented pupils have special needs that we must cater for. How can we prevent them from becoming disillusioned?

- [ ] What constitutes good progress for gifted and talented pupils?

- [ ] How do we ensure more effective differentiation for gifted and talented pupils?

- [ ] How should we approach the four attainment targets?

- [ ] How can we structure our classroom teaching to engage gifted and talented pupils without alienating less able pupils?

- [ ] What are meaningful extension activities?

- [ ] What about homework?

chapter 2

Gifted and talented pupils have special needs that we must cater for. How can we prevent them from becoming disillusioned?

Gifted and talented pupils can be challenging, particularly with regard to our methodology. Gifted and talented pupils are sometimes identified as being 'arrogant' and interestingly enough 'lazy', often because they are reluctant to jump through hoops which they deem unnecessary. Their approach to some tasks, which they feel are almost beneath their intelligence, can be challenging in the extreme, particularly in a whole-class situation. It is therefore important that, as professionals, we take care not to dismiss such challenges but rather to examine our own approach to our teaching and consider how to rise to the challenge of appropriate differentiation. Perhaps we aren't stretching these pupils enough. Are we just giving them 'more of the same', i.e. tasks that they have already completed in a third of the time of anyone else? We need to tailor our approach to their needs. If we do this, we may find that those gifted and talented children, who may formerly have questioned the approach, become absorbed in challenging tasks, and become invaluable contributors to our lessons.

It is essential that we view the needs of these pupils as a challenge that we can meet, rather than a threat to ourselves personally.

What constitutes good progress for gifted and talented pupils?

So what types of work should they be doing? And how can that dovetail with day-to-day language teaching?

According to observation by OFSTED, good progress in language learning means that pupils can:

- apply their knowledge in a wider range of practical situations;
- increasingly take the initiative, ask questions and offer comment and justify their opinions more fully;

- show greater understanding of the grammatical structures of the language and greater accuracy in their use;
- expand their vocabulary to deal with different subject areas;
- learn how to use their existing knowledge to best effect in coping with the unfamiliar;
- develop independence in completing tasks and using reference sources.

(Alan Dobson, HMI – CILT Secondary Languages Show, November 2000)

If we bear these features of good progress in mind, we can come to a better understanding of how to improve our methodology, for all our pupils.

We must also be aware of the nature of tasks that we require pupils to complete on a daily basis. Are they fostering the aptitudes outlined above, or are we aiming at a narrow, more restrictive skill set?

How do we ensure more effective differentiation for gifted and talented pupils?

It is helpful to redefine ways of differentiating at this point:

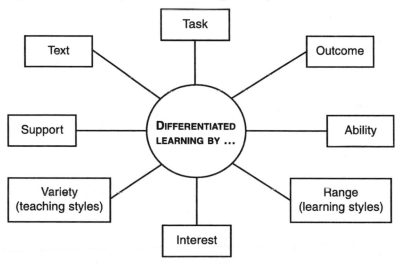

Source: Convery and Coyle 1999

Differentiation is a word which strikes fear into the hearts of many language teachers. At conferences I have attended across the country, I have never once met a language teacher who has expressed satisfaction with his or her differentiation! But I think, as ever, we are being too hard on ourselves. Differentiation by outcome is a perfectly valid means of differentiation if the tasks are appropriate. It is also important to note that pupils of different abilities do not need to be doing different work **all** of the time. Secondly, the notion of 'core' work and branch planning is a useful timesaver. This book aims to suggest painless ways of rising to the challenge.

Within the framework of differentiation, we need to consider what type of tasks more able pupils should be doing and in which contexts. This is where an understanding of cognitive challenge comes into play.

> *Cummins distinguished between two different types of communication: BICS and CALP. BICS constitute basic interpersonal communication skills, which a learner needs in order to function in a daily interpersonal context, usually in face-to-face communication with lots of non-verbal cues. CALP is to do with acquiring cognitive academic learning proficiency, where a learner is able to reflect on the surface features of language outside the immediate environment, typically in an academic context. Such a setting makes major cognitive demands on the learner, usually in the absence of paralinguistic and situational cues. The division is a useful one, since it allowsp teachers to consider the appropriateness and the contextual significance of different tasks they are planning for their learners.* (Coyle in Masih 1999: 49)

(Do Coyle in her article 'Supporting students in CLIL contexts' in *Learning through a foreign language: models, methods and outcomes* (ed John Masih)

Where do the tasks and activities that we ask our pupils to undertake fall in relation to this grid? Often, language tasks fall below the middle line, either 'context-embedded' or 'context-unembedded'. We require our learners to mimic, to parrot, to copy. We require them to identify or put in order in reading and listening tasks. We require them to match up.

High cognitive demand

Context-embedded	Context-unembedded

Generalises

Compares and **contrasts** ideas

Summarises

Plans

Classifies by known criteria

Transforms, personalises, gives information

Recalls and **reviews**

Seeks solutions to problems

Argues a case using evidence persuasively

Identifies criteria, **develops** and **sustains**

Justifies opinion or judgement

Evaluates critically

Interprets evidence, makes deductions

Forms hypotheses, asks further questions for investigation

Predicts results

Applies principles to new situation

Analyses, suggests solution and tests

Context-embedded —— (COGNITIVE PROCESSES) —— Context-unembedded

Reading to find specific information
- identifies
- names
- matches
- retells

Transfers information from one medium to another

Applies known procedures

Describes observations

Sequences

Narrates with sense of beginning, middle, end

- **Parrots**: repeats utterances of adult or peer

- **Copies**: reproduces information from board or text

Low cognitive demand

Differentiation and individual learners – Cummins in Hall, 1995

The realisation that many of tasks are of low cognitive demand goes a long way to explaining challenging behaviour on the part of gifted and talented pupils. We need therefore to define the types of tasks that **will** engage our pupils. We should be looking for a different order of things to do rather than just comprehension/answering questions/identifying/ordering.

Do Coyle, (ibid, p53) goes on to outline what she terms the four Cs:

CONTENT – PROGRESSION

COGNITION – ENGAGEMENT

COMMUNICATION – INTERACTION

CULTURE – AWARENESS

She suggests that:

> it is through **progression** in the knowledge, skills and understanding
> of the content, by **engagement** in associated cognitive processing,
> **interaction** in the communicative context, and a deepening **awareness**
> and positioning of self and otherness, that learning takes place.

An understanding of this thinking and a willingness to review our pedagogy in the light of it is crucial if we are to engage more able pupils fully in the classroom.

Teaching styles and learning styles will be discussed further in Chapter 4.

How should we approach the four attainment targets?

What kind of tasks, then, could we be looking at setting in the different **attainment targets**?

We should consider the importance of varying our approach across the skills from the beginning of Key Stage 3.

AT1

Listening tasks are often perceived as tests. The learner is often much less interested in the message than in acquiring a tick for a right answer. Listening has become more a testing than a teaching activity. Tasks can also be closed and lacking in cognitive challenge. What can we do about this?

Routine has a role to play here, and teacher confidence is crucial in being able to set up different listening tasks at any one time. Less able learners might be completing an ordering task, while the more able are required to focus on 'core language'.

These tasks might prove motivating:
• encouraging prediction;
• pre-listening activities based on key language;
• asking pupils to listen for different words that they already know and to indicate when they have heard them (or what precedes or follows them);
• using transcriptions to focus on grammar or the sound–spelling relationship;
• asking pupils to infer meaning and emotion;
• identifying 'who what where when';
• asking more able pupils to generate or create language using a listening task as a stimulus;
• matching the content of our texts to the maturity level of our pupils.

Consider the following GCSE task, where the input consists of fairly adult vocabulary, which could subsequently lead to open-ended oral work. This type of material immediately requires an opinion from a more able learner, a degree of personal involvement.

5 *La dépendance*

Discussing addiction

* * * * * * * * * *

1a Écoutez les opinions de ces jeunes et décidez qui parle.

C'est adulte de fumer.

Ça pue, je n'aime pas!

Si on fume à proximité des enfants, c'est pas bon.

Ahmed

Alicia

Sylvie

C'est jeter l'argent par les fenêtres.

Je fume pour me décrisper.

Élodie

Sabrina

Les cigarettes me donnent confiance en moi.

Hervé

Si on fume, on risque d'avoir un cancer du poumon.

Elsa

On est vite dépendant! Après, c'est difficile de laisser tomber!

François

C'est agréable de fumer une clope avec ses copains.

Yolande

une clope	*a fag*
se décrisper	*to relax*

une maladie cardio-vasculaire	*heart disease*

1b Faites un sondage auprès de votre classe.
Posez les questions suivantes:

Est-ce que vous fumez? Pourquoi? Pourquoi pas?

1c À deux. En français:

Je suis pour/contre les cigarettes
I am for/against cigarettes

A
- Say you are against cigarettes
- Say that they are very expensive
- Say you risk cancer and heart disease
- Say you don't smoke

B
- Say you are for cigarettes
- Say you look more grown-up if you smoke
- Say it gives you more self-confidence if you have a cigarette in your hand
- Say you smoke three cigarettes a day

158 cent cinquante-huit

Vous avez vu ces images dans un magazine.
Qu'en pensez-vous? Écrivez en français au magazine.
Répondez à ces questions:

Pourquoi est-ce que les jeunes fument?
Est-ce que vous fumez? Pourquoi, pourquoi pas?
Décrivez une soirée récente où beaucoup de gens fumaient.

2a Écoutez ces publicités. (1–4)
Elles sont de la part de quelle
organisation?

2b Lisez le texte et répondez aux questions.

Quel est le risque le plus grave pour notre santé au 21ème siècle?

Pour moi, c'est fumer. Les jeunes connaissent les risques du cancer, il y a même une annonce sur les paquets de cigarettes, mais ils s'en fichent, parce qu'ils pensent que c'est cool de fumer. Il faut être comme ses copains. À mon avis, c'est plutôt stupide.
Manon, 16 ans

Je pense que l'alcool est très dangereux. C'est une drogue, mais tout le monde en boit, même les parents à la maison. On ne sait pas ce qu'on fait quand on a trop bu, et ça, c'est très mauvais.

Quand j'avais seize ans, je fumais vingt clopes par jour. Je buvais presque tous les jours aussi, une ou deux bières, le vendredi soir du whisky-coca ou du cidre. Je faisais ça pour impressionner les autres. Au bout d'un moment, je me suis rendu compte que je fumais trop et que je devais m'arrêter. J'ai donc évité le cancer du poumon.
Daniel, 27 ans

Surtout parmi les jeunes filles, les maladies comme l'anorexie et la boulimie sont pénibles. Les magazines et la télé insistent qu'il faut être à la mode, populaire, et mince. Beaucoup de jeunes souffrent à cause de ça.
Marie-Jo, 15 ans

Qui pense que/qu':

a les médias encouragent les maladies alimentaires?
b on fume sans y penser
c si on boit trop, on ne sait pas ce qu'on fait?
d on fume pour être cool?
e on est influencé par ses parents à boire de l'alcool?
f on est influencé par ses camarades de classe à fumer?

Rappel

The imperfect tense can also be used to mean *used to*:
Je buvais presque tous les jours.
I used to drink nearly every day.
Je fumais vingt clopes par jour.
I used to smoke 20 fags per day.
See page 208

cent cinquante-neuf **159**

Source: *Métro 4* by Anneli McLachlan (© Heinemann, 2001)

Follow-up activity

Tu es d'accord ou tu n'es pas d'accord? Donne des raisons à ta réponse.

Before undertaking the survey suggested, pupils could predict the opinions they expected to hear and predict the overall results of the survey.

Such a task moves us on towards higher cognitive demand by personalising, by predicting and by forming hypotheses.

Listening transcripts are perhaps underused as a means of introducing vocabulary and focusing attention, and also as a means of highlighting grammatical points and underlining the sound–spelling relationship. Gifted and talented pupils often find it particularly motivating to see exactly what is being said.

AT2

Tasks which involve real communication, tasks where interaction is involved and where the learner is interested in the message promote learning. Too often, the oral tasks we set are of little import to our learners. All pupils feel this, but the shortcomings of such tasks are acutely felt by the gifted and talented. What can we do about this?

We can encourage our pupils to say more. Pupils, particularly the more able, want to be free to say what they want to say, rather than producing what we want them to say. They seek to broaden, not to restrict. They wish to make and generate sentences. They seek to understand how language works and are then ready to transfer it. This of course requires support, which might come in the shape of scaffolding or speaking frames. It also requires input, but questions the process whereby teacher input aims to produce identical output. A degree of engagement and personalisation is needed.

As well as topic-based vocabulary, pupils need to be taught from the outset 'core' language – opinion-giving vocabulary. They need to be exposed to open-ended questions as part of classroom routine. They need also to develop an awareness of how to expand their utterances and how to develop quality. All this needs to be taught. They should meet, absorb and manipulate language.

What exactly are they talking about? Is it intrinsically of interest to them? Or is it somehow sterile or distant from their experience? These are the questions which need to be raised.

The following tasks, all aimed at Key Stage 3 pupils, allow for a degree of opinion and involvement that perhaps an information gap task on places to meet or expressions of quantity does not. They have the interest factor on their side too.

Task 1 – Giving opinions

A picture of Posh Spice or any other celebrity provides a stimulus here. The core language is highlighted for less able pupils. The questions are revealed one at a time and answers accepted from around the class. Requests for vocabulary are given and noted down. The task requires a personal response and ends with a pairwork exercise on questions – 'If you met X, what would you ask him/her?'. The logical follow-up to this task would be for pupils to become the teacher in subsequent lessons, to find their own pictures and to ask for opinions.

Qui c'est?

Comment est-elle?

Qu'est-ce qu'elle porte?

Est-ce que tu aimes ses vêtements?

J'aime _____ mais je n'aime pas _____ , c'est _____ .

Si tu rencontrais Posh Spice – quelles questions poserais-tu?

This Posh Spice task allows pupils to search for their own adjectives to describe the singer. It personalises the language they are using and allows them a positive or negative reaction. Gifted and talented pupils seek out such opportunities to react and personalise.

Getting into routines, using similar tasks on a regular basis, will give all pupils confidence and engage their interest. Display can be used to reinforce language. Rather than being prescriptive, or expecting an answer that is right or wrong, opening things up in this way and including an element of choice moves all pupils towards spontaneous use of language.

The use of display can be vital in helping pupils to transfer language, but first and foremost, the teacher must be on the ball and can help to show how structures are not confined to any one context, but are dynamic and exciting and flexible. Gifted and talented pupils can certainly be used as a teaching aid within this context.

Task 2 – Using video clips to promote opinions

Most pupils love working with videos. The following activity consists of a short burst of any film – two minutes maximum – and invites a personal response, providing a framework of support. All the boxes are designed to be overlaid on transparencies.

Pupils watch the clip twice, then give a one word reaction from box 1.

They then extend their utterance using box 2. They expand their utterance by inserting an adverb from box 3. Their partner then reacts by choosing an opinion from box 4. This involves – we hope – real interaction and opinions and real learning. Gifted and talented pupils respond particularly well because of the open nature of this task. They may also have suggestions to make regarding the content of the boxes …

Box 1	Box 2	Box 3	Box 4
affreux	*C'était ...*	*très*	*Ah bon?*
bizarre			
chouette		*trop*	*Ah oui?*
cool			
ennuyeux	*Je l'ai trouvé ...*	*vraiment*	*Ah non!*
extra			
fantastique		*totalement*	*Pas pour moi!*
formidable			
génial	*A mon avis,*		*Penses-tu?*
nul	*c'était ...*		

Task 3 – Using pictures

Picture routine can be successfully used in the MFL classroom to elicit a personal response and to add a degree of unpredictability. Pupils can choose the questions they wish to answer or the teacher can differentiate appropriately. Used on a regular basis and reinforced by classroom display, picture use will improve general expression, opinion giving and use of core language. Gifted and talented pupils can be encouraged to become teachers of such routines.

- Name something in the picture
- Describe it – say what's happening
- Say if you like or dislike something in the picture
- Say what you think a person is saying
- Imagine a conversation between the people – if there's more than one person!
- Say what happened before the picture
- Say what happened after the picture
- Say what a person might be thinking
- Make up three questions about the picture

(With thanks to Mini-Flashcard Language Games)

The following tasks might also usefully be given prominence in oral work in the classroom in order to engage gifted and talented pupils:

- pronunciation practice – reading out loud;
- asking questions;
- dealing with the unpredictable;
- playing for time;
- transferring language from one context to another.

AT3

For reading to be successful for our more able pupils, we need to think about the nature of the texts we are offering. Which quadrant of our BICS-CALP diagram do they fall in? (See page 21.) Are we offering longer chunks, which are denser in meaning with more demanding tasks? We also need to consider for what purpose we are asking our pupils to read.

Including the following activities in AT3 practice will bear fruit for the gifted and talented:

- prediction;
- skimming and scanning;
- reading for gist;
- making links between different types of words;
- finding clues;
- identifying patterns.

The following worksheet extends a normal classroom activity to demonstrate how these reading activities can be adapted to fit in with everyday working patterns.

Of course an open-ended activity is also needed here. For example: *Est-ce que tu aimerais rencontrer Patrice? Pourquoi? Pourquoi pas?*

We will consider extended reading in Chapter 4.

EN PLUS *Lettre de mon corres*

 1a Qui est-ce?

 1b Vrai ou faux?
True or false?

1 Patrice est français.
2 Il habite à Chantilly.
3 Chantilly est en Suisse.
4 Patrice a les cheveux bruns.
5 Il est paresseux.
6 Il n'a pas de frère.
7 Le chat s'appelle Gilles.
8 Le chien s'appelle Milou.
9 Gilles a 15 ans.
10 Clémentine a 8 ans.

Salut!

Je m'appelle Patrice Meugeot. J'ai douze ans. Mon anniversaire, c'est le 15 juillet. Je suis français. J'habite en France, à Chantilly, près de Paris. J'ai les cheveux blonds et courts et les yeux noisette. Je suis sportif et bavard.

J'ai un frère et deux sœurs. Mon frère s'appelle Gilles. Il a les yeux bleus et les cheveux châtains. Il a seize ans. Mes sœurs s'appellent Clémentine et Anne-Laure. Clémentine a huit ans. Elle a un chat qui s'appelle Pouchka. Anne-Laure a quatre ans. Elle a un chien qui s'appelle Milou.

 1c Qui parle? Écoute et note. (1–4)

36 trente-six

Source: *Métro 1* by Rosi McNab (© Heinemann, 1999)

Prediction

Lettre de mon corres

What is this letter going to be about?

■ Skimming and scanning

In which line does Patrice talk about:

a – where he lives _____

b – his brother _____

c – his sisters' pets _____

■ Un peu de lecture

Avec un partenaire, lis la lettre à haute voix.

(With your partner, take it in turns to read through the letter out loud in French.)

Task 1a – Qui est-ce?

Look at the pictures, what clues do you think you are being given? Discuss this with your partner.

_____

_____

■ Making links between different types of words

Quel est le lien?

(What do each set of words have in common?)

a – je m'appelle, j'ai, je suis, j'habite, il a, elle a _____

b – Patrice, France, Chantilly, Paris, Clémentine, Anne-Laure, Pouchka, Milou _____

c – blonds, courts, noisette, sportif, bavard _____

d – Gilles – il, Clémentine – elle _____

■ Identifying patterns

Remplis les trous! (Fill in the gaps!)

Je m'appell____   Il s'appell____

J'habit____   Elle s'appell____

Task 1b – Vrai ou faux?

Si les phrases sont fausses, écris une phrase vraie.

(True or false? If the sentences are false, write a correct sentence.)

AT4

For writing to be successful for our more able pupils, we need to think about the nature of the tasks we are offering. Writing can be a creative, liberating experience, offering pupils the opportunity to apply imagination and also to work independently and use reference materials. But writing tasks too often consist of replacing words or phrases within a model. This type of task spells demotivation for a more able pupil.

We could consider using the following approaches:

- Using different stimuli – would our more able pupils respond better to pictures or poems?
- What is their motivation to write? Is there real communication going on, or is the task mechanical?
- What about changing the context, choosing crazy themes?
- We can use writing frames as a scaffold, provide form, e.g. poems, for them to transform.
- We can require oral exploitation of written work.

The following writing frame provides essential structures and guidance on content in English, while allowing gifted and talented pupils sufficient freedom to express opinions and take the comparison in the direction they wish to follow.

Comparing schools

Name _____ Date _____

Introduce yourself and your school briefly – which town and country is your school in?	*Je suis élève au collège* *C'est à* *en / au*
Which days do you go to school? And in the other country?	*Nous allons à l'école* *Mais en / au / aux / à la / à l'* *on va à l'école*
What time do you start school? And in the other country?	*Nous commençons à heures.* *Mais en / au / aux / à la / à l'* *on commence à heures.*
Which subjects do you study? And in the other country?	*Nous étudions* *Mais en / au / aux / à la / à l'* *on étudie*
At what age did you start French? And when do they start English in the other country?	*Nous commençons le français à l'âge de* *Mais en / au / aux / à la / à l'* *on commence l'anglais à l'âge de*
What and where do you eat at lunch-time? And in the other country?	*A midi, nous mangeons* *Mais en / au / aux / à la / à l'* *on mange*
What sports do you do at school? And in the other country?	*Nous faisons du sport à l'école, par exemple* *Mais en / au / aux / à la / à l'* *on*
Which country would you prefer to go to school in? Why?	*Je préférerais être élève en / au / aux / à la / à l'* *parce que*

Source: *French writing frames: Creative and imaginative writing* by Julie Adams
(© Folens, 2000)

How can we structure our classroom teaching to engage gifted and talented pupils without alienating less able pupils?

Questioning techniques lie at the heart of the answer to this question. It is often at the presentational oral stage that our most able may switch off. How can we ensure that we command and retain their full attention?

Many of us have been trained to use three-stage questioning in order to build up to an answer:

stage one – yes/no questions;
stage two – alternative questions;
stage three – open questions.

Such an approach has its merits and its place, but there has always been a notion that we should proceed religiously through the stages. Such an approach does not absorb gifted pupils, who very soon realise that they can miss out stages as they may well master the vocabulary or structures on offer before others. It is important to hold everyone's interest if input is to be of use. We can, therefore, consider adopting a less predictable questioning routine which is nonetheless tailored to individual pupils – in short, we can offer our more able pupils a more challenging question early on to ensure their engagement.

Here is a very simple example in Spanish:

Aim of lesson
To practise *tener* singular and adjectival agreements. Pupils have learnt the adjectives for colour of hair and eyes. This lesson is concentrating particularly on the core language *tengo, tienes, tiene*. Extension for the more able can come via inclusion of opinions *opino yo que es muy feo/fea, guapo/guapa* and also by using *tendría* for one's ideal partner.

La mujer tiene el pelo rojo y los ojos azules.

Questioning might normally proceed:

Stage 1   *¿Tiene el pelo rojo? Sí o no?*
¿Tiene los ojos verdes? Sí o no?

Stage 2   *¿Tiene el pelo rojo o el pelo negro?*
¿Tiene los ojos verdes o los ojos azules?

Stage 3   *Describe la mujer.*

Our more able pupils may well be able to describe the woman immediately after hearing our input. They may then switch off during the oral work. If we have identified them we can keep their attention by firing stage 3 questions at them and also by extending the context further and adding such questions as:

¿Puedes describir tu profesor de ciencias? ¿Cómo se llama? ¿Cómo es? ¿Te gusta tu profesor de ciencias? ¿Porqué? ¿Es guapo o feo?

¿Tu compañero ideal – cómo sería? Supplying *tendría*.

It is worth adding at this point that there is no reason why we can't focus our questioning on the structures, proposing rogue verbs:

¿ Tiene los ojos azules o come los ojos azules?

¿ Tiene los ojos azules o tengo los ojos azules?

Topic-based approaches sadly neglect these possibilities, so that pupils learn too many nouns and too few coathangers on which to hang them. We can go some way to remedying this situation by shifting the focus within our teaching, making pupils aware of core language from the outset, rather than adopting a noun-saturated approach.

What are meaningful extension activities?

We need to ask ourselves what we are requiring of our pupils. Are the tasks too easy for them? In our planning, whenever we approach a lesson we can ask what type of tasks as outlined in the four attainment targets above we could painlessly add to extend our most able pupils. How can we get them to transfer their knowledge? What tasks can we ask them to do which will involve imagination and creativity? How can we move them on to justifying, hypothesising, problem-solving?

If we find answers to these questions and include such activities in our planning, then we are providing meaningful extension activities. Our gifted and talented pupils need such challenging, open-ended tasks, not more of the same.

What about homework?

Homework is another domain where more able pupils perhaps switch off because the task may be repetitive and undemanding. One way of avoiding this scenario is by adding an element of choice. While gap-fills and rehearsing of conversations might be suitable for some, the more able are more likely to rise to the challenge if there is an element of choice and a degree of creativity. Some schools set homework via departmental sheets where a pupil can choose an activity, which will help him or her to practise the structures or vocabulary on offer.

Speaking homeworks are often successful and the following are generally well received:

- preparing for a presentation;
- practising using cuecards;
- teaching someone what he or she has learnt in class;
- pronunciation practice;

- making tapes;
- using walkmans for listening homeworks;
- creating little books (see Pathfinder 40: *Just write!* p62 by Adams and Panter);
- making games;
- making cards;
- making chatterboxes;
- extended reading (see Chapter 4);
- computer club tasks;
- poems – concrete words/acrostic poems;
- brainstorming what they want to learn in this unit.

There is a very useful Pathfinder 20 – *Nightshift: ideas and strategies for homework*, which takes this subject further.

key points	• **We should avoid giving gifted and talented pupils more of the same**
	• **We should provide tasks that constitute a cognitive challenge**
	• **We can usefully review our approach to the four ATs, placing the emphasis on manipulation, generation and creativity**

Learning to learn

□ Are our pupils doing enough of the learning?

□ How can we use our gifted and talented pupils to help with teaching learning strategies?

□ How can we make sure our pupils learn to work independently?

□ How do we get them working together?

□ How do we create a secure environment for risk-takers?

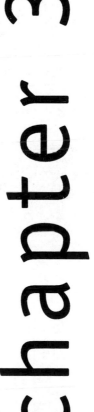

Are our pupils doing enough of the learning?

Effective differentiation affects teaching styles and learning styles. We acknowledge that all pupils learn in different ways: consequently, there are implications for our teaching styles. This is particularly to the fore where gifted and talented pupils are concerned. There is also a national concern that our pupils' study habits are not as well developed as they could be across the board. With respect to languages, at the CILT Secondary Languages Show in November 2000, HMI Alan Dobson raised the following questions:

- Do our pupils strive to express new notions in the target language, re-using previously learnt language?
- How systematically do pupils note new language and commit it to memory?
- How effectively do they use reference sources?

If we can find ways of ensuring that our answers to these questions are positive, then we are encouraging our pupils to do their fair share of learning. The challenge to get pupils to re-use previously learnt language occurs every day. (See p49 of this chapter for some ideas on how to move pupils forward. Study skills and routines, including noting of new language and use of reference sources, are also discussed in this chapter.)

At the same time, we should examine our teaching. Are we inputting madly and simply delighted when a pupil utters one word? We need to look to learner-centred possibilities. We need to give our pupils the will and the wherewithal to perform. Gifted and talented pupils will rise to the challenge.

How can we use our gifted and talented pupils to help with teaching learning strategies?

It is essential to recognise, however, that while gifted and talented pupils may well be able to articulate their preferred learning style, it is important that we teach learning strategies explicitly. (See Pathfinder 31: *Teaching learners how to learn* pp11–15.)

Teachers make assumptions about the skills that learners bring to lessons, where often the assumption needs to be made for most pupils that we are in fact starting from scratch.

Learning strategies need to be planned into our schemes of work and given space in all Key Stages. Our gifted and talented pupils are particularly useful in the classroom context as they can articulate how they learn. Their own repertoire of learning strategies must not be neglected, however. Indeed, it is a teacher's duty to ensure that they expand their range of approaches.

In a Year 6 masterclass that I taught involving Year 6 pupils from six primary schools, the scheme of work was designed to cover learning strategies in three languages. One of the first activities was to set, as homework, a number of sentences to be learnt by heart. At the beginning of the next lesson, the first activity was for the class to share learning strategies. A vast range of sophisticated strategies had been used and the learning experience of all the gifted and talented pupils enabled them to note down different things to try and thus to expand their repertoire. Some pupils had used lists, others mind maps. Some had invented games, some had involved their parents. Others had invented mnemonics. They showed a vast range of learning styles and an equally vast range of learning strategies.

In the same way, more able pupils will make explicit the strategies that they find useful, helping the whole class to follow their example. Not just in learning vocabulary, but in how to use reference materials, tackle listening tasks, skim read, write to include opinions – right from the start.

The overview scheme of work for the masterclass is featured overleaf.

Week beginning:	Strategies/grammar/activities	Context
French module		
Week 1	Memorisation techniques – word association/spider diagrams	School subjects
Week 2	Memorisation techniques – songs/rhymes/mnemonics	School subjects
Week 3	Gender	School subjects
Week 4	Adjectival agreement	School subjects
Week 5	*Faire du/de la*	School subjects/days
Week 6	Using verb tables	Pot pourri
Week 7	Negatives	Pot pourri
Week 8	Tenses – using *aller*	Countries
Week 9	Drama workshop	Consolidation
Week 10	Predicting	What people study and why
Week 11	Breaking down streams of sound	Timetables
Week 12	Listening for gist	Holiday plans
Week 13	Checking for accuracy	Holidays
Week 14	Using all-purpose words	Holidays/school
German module		
Week 1	Communication strategies/fillers	Everyday conversation
Week 2	Gender	Family
Week 3	Plurals	Family
Week 4	Cases/*kein*	Animals
Week 5	Analysing unknown words	Pot pourri
Week 6	Word order	Character
Week 7	Word order	Character
Week 8	Formal and informal language	Interviews
Week 9	*Gern/nicht gern*	Likes/dislikes
Week 10	Technology workshop	

How can we make sure our pupils learn to work independently?

Some able pupils' preferred learning style is a solitary one. In this case, it is our job to expand their repertoire and offer them possibilities for social interaction. They need to be allocated a particular role within group work. Their range of strategies will therefore expand.

In order for all our pupils to work independently with success, learning strategies obviously need to be covered in depth. They include many skill-specific strategies (see Pathfinder 31: *Teaching learners how to learn* pp7–8) and also the following:

■ **Memorising – the envelope technique is useful here!**

Whatever is being learnt: a new verb, a new lexical field, examples of a grammatical structure, we can encourage pupils to make (and store!) learning envelopes. This can be done in class and set for homework at all levels. They are ideal for revision. Gifted and talented pupils need to be made aware of the need for review and revision. The envelope technique encourages good habits from the outset. Consider the example below.

ich komme	I come/I am coming
du kommst	you (fam. sing.) come/you are coming
er kommt	he comes/he is coming
sie kommt	she comes/she is coming
es kommt	it comes/it is coming
wir kommen	we come/we are coming
ihr kommt	you (fam. pl.) come/you are coming
Sie kommen	you (formal, sing./pl.) come/you are coming
sie kommen	they come/they are coming

The sheet is produced and then cut up so that pupils can practise matching up meaning at home. Pupils do the cutting in their own time.

This KS3 task assumes familiarity with conjugation and also with some grammatical abbreviations. These have obviously been discussed and taught previously, and are indeed a regular feature of lessons. In the noting down of vocabulary, the teacher needs to be on the ball, checking copywriting and progress. Crib sheets may need to be provided for less able pupils to ensure a correct complete version. Initially, teachers might want to provide photocopied envelope fodder until their pupils have got the hang of this routine.

Differentiation then becomes easy. Meaning can be practised, verb endings, etc. The important thing is to ensure that pupils also have some means of checking their learning, perhaps in their own vocabulary or grammar books. The fun approach and kinaesthetic nature of this task has meant that subsequent use of the structures or vocabulary set for learning has been much more successful than the 'learn these words for homework' approach.

Other strategies for memorising include setting the learning as a particular task.

'I want you to learn these words by:

- writing two sentences containing each word;
- using 'look, cover, say';
- requiring a physical response for phrases;
- trying word association;
- writing an acrostic ...'

Higher order tasks to expand vocabulary include finding synonyms for phrases and different ways of saying things. Some pupils learn better by using semantic maps, which can subsequently be displayed in class. Requiring a visual reponse is often rewarding. This verb machine was created by a pupil at Elliott School:

If finances permit, the simple addition of a very small grammar/vocabulary book and discussion of how vocabulary and structures should be noted will lend weight to learning strategies. What abbreviations should be used? Should each new structure or word also appear as a discrete item as well as in a sentence?

■ Dictionary skills

Gifted and talented pupils need to acquire early on the skills that they need to become independent language learners. In all pupils, these are often taken for granted and are crucial in the development of independent language learners. Whilst gifted and talented pupils' skills may be more advanced than their peers, there is generally room for improvement here. Elimination of glaringly bad dictionary use in Year 7 pays dividends in later years and leads to independence. When pupils are working things out for themselves, they are doing the learning, they are developing autonomy. We must encourage this to happen, so that they can operate independently.

The example on page 46 is taken from Collins Easy Learning Dictionaries. These dictionaries are designed to encourage dictionary skills and language awareness. Focusing on such aspects brings us more independent learners with more strategies at their disposal.

■ Game creation

A nice open-ended creative task requires pupils to create a game to activate what they have learnt in a particular unit. This type of activity allows learners to personalise their work and gives their creativity free rein – ideally suited for more able children.

WORDGAME 2

▶ PARTS OF SPEECH ◀

In each sentence below a word has been shaded. Put a tick in the appropriate box to show whether it's a **noun**, **adjective**, **adverb** or **verb** each time. Look in the section "Dictionary Skills" at the front of the book to remind you what nouns, adjectives, adverbs and verbs are. Remember, there may be more than one entry for each word.

SENTENCE	NOUN	ADJ	ADV	VERB
1. La ferme de mes parents est en Alsace.				
2. Il n'est pas franc.				
3. Le magasin ferme dans deux minutes.				
4. Le dîner est à 20 heures.				
5. Tu veux goûter ma mousse au chocolat?				
6. Je n'aime pas la bière.				
7. C'est un faux passeport.				
8. J'entends des pas dans l'escalier.				
9. Ce film nous a fait rire.				
10. Cette voiture est mal garée.				

Source: Reproduced from Collins French Easy Learning Dictionary with the permission of HarperCollins Publishers Ltd (© HarperCollins Ltd 2001)

■ **Strategies for checking work**

Our pupils are notoriously bad at checking their work, gifted and talented learners also. Why is this? How can we teach them to do it better? There are no hard and fast answers to these questions. The National Literacy Framework will offer much-needed support for language teachers, but it remains evident that we must put accuracy, in speaking, listening, reading and writing, high on the agenda from the outset. Establishing good habits in Key Stage 3 is therefore essential. Writing can be an extremely good source of group work, which results in collaborative checking strategies to inform pupils' own practice. Gifted and talented pupils have much to input here.

Pupils can:
• write together on any theme, with results shared and critiqued on the OHP;
• write together in the computer room and change computer to carry on with each other's narrative;
• learn to record vocabulary and structures in a particular way and be encouraged to indicate in their written work when they have referred to their notes.

Running dictation allows teachers to allocate roles to differentiate effectively. More able pupils can be the scribes or the runners or they can police other groups' answers.

Teachers can:
• reward elaborate phrases;
• set AT4 specific targets to improve pupils' performance.

How do we get them working together?

Some gifted and talented pupils prefer to work alone. As I have stated earlier in this chapter, it is important that they learn to work with others. All pupils benefit from group work. Teachers may wish to group pupils by ability depending on the nature of the task. We can consider providing our gifted and talented pupils with group challenges in all four skills as well as involving them in content choice. Their task might consist of a research-based project culminating in an oral presentation and a written display. Collaborative work ensures pupils learn from each other, bouncing ideas and language off each other, as well as working towards an outcome which the classroom teacher can subsequently exploit for others in the class.

Reading is a skill which is frequently neglected as something that can be done well in groups. A useful routine to adopt might be the following:

- Predict what the passage is about.
- Read through the passage.
- Underline all the words you know.
- Underline the words that you think you can guess.
- Note down how you've come to this conclusion.
- Respond to the questions: who what where when?
- Tackle the questions set.
- Write definitions in the TL of five words that figure in the passage.
- Formulate five questions on the passage.
- Write a creative response.

Such routines built into our teaching programmes provide gifted and talented pupils with tools to tackle denser passages, which are perhaps less context-embedded and therefore more challenging.

To a certain extent, MFL is the odd subject out! Pupils come to us from primary school used to working together. They work on history research together. They work on drama improvisation together. They work on science experiments together. They work on English presentations in groups. In the next chapter we will see that pupils want to have the opportunity to work together.

How do we create a secure environment for risk-takers?

Language is dynamic. Pupils perceive languages as being difficult and also being starkly right and wrong, whereas in other subjects where subjectivity plays a greater role – English, History – they feel less exposed, perhaps. Teaching different structures and synonyms is important so that pupils feel that there are alternative means of expression. Teacher input is not the sole model. Similarly, teaching pupils to be able to cope with what they know and to get round situations leads to a feeling of security – in short, actively teaching communication strategies. More able pupils will make more use of communication strategies than others. This demands a certain flexibility and confidence on the part of the teacher, a willingness to depart from the strictures of the syllabus. We must create a secure environment for our able risk-takers.

For all pupils to feel secure, we must also question our attitudes to mistakes. I have stated above that accuracy is of the utmost importance, but do we over-react sometimes? Are there circumstances where message and originality can win out over grammatical accuracy? This is not to advocate sloppiness – correct pronunciation and grammatical accuracy have a role to play – but we could establish a system of rewards for adventurous use of language.

I had a wallchart where I rewarded pupils for particularly impressive phrases at GCSE German. The class vied to receive their stamps and this system encouraged them to depart from stock phrases and be more creative with their language. Gifted and talented pupils took the lead. Such reward systems foster creativity and originality; they encourage pupils to have a go rather than to think that they must always be 100% correct in their utterances.

Risk-takers can also benefit if beginnings of lessons are used to help pupils make sense of their learning and put things together, to be able to transfer language from one context to another. I would often start Year 8 German with revision designed to practise a range of grammatical points across different topics, actively encouraging pupils to be a bit quirky. This would include some visual stimuli, but also straightforward sentence-building. For example:

Wie sagt man 'He is coming' *auf Deutsch?*
Wie sagt man 'tomorrow' *auf Deutsch?*
Wie sagt man 'He is coming tomorrow'?
Gibt es eine andere Möglichkeit? (Looking for an inverted sentence – supported by display.)
Wie sagt man 'The ice man is coming tomorrow'?

A note about display. The extent of the role of classroom display should not be underestimated. It affords links, support, helps us to show the difference if used properly. Teachers or even more able pupils can institute a phrase of the week, a tense of the week, a verb of the week and pupils can gain points every time they use it. This is all part of encouraging fun and creativity rather than imposing a regular pattern on children. They invariably rise to the challenge and the humorous creative use of language I referred to in Chapter 1 often results.

key points	• Even gifted and talented pupils need to be taught how to learn
	• Gifted and talented pupils can show others the way forward with learning strategies
	• Group work can be of immense benefit to gifted and talented pupils
	• Getting pupils to do more of the work should be a key aim of our teaching

Broadening our outlook

- [ ] What do able pupils want?

- [ ] What about grammar?

- [ ] Are our pupils stimulated by the materials we choose?

- [ ] How can we engage their interest?

- [ ] What about ICT?

chapter 4

What do able pupils want?

I considered in Chapter 3 the enjoyment and satisfaction that all pupils, but especially gifted and talented pupils, derive from personalising language, from creating their own utterances, synthesising and generating, rather than parroting (see page 21). Linda Fisher, senior lecturer in Modern Languages at Homerton College, Cambridge, has undertaken some fascinating research among Year 12 pupils, who were Higher candidates at GCSE and who may or may not be studying languages in Year 12. She asked them how they thought their studies could be improved. As Higher candidates, many of those questioned would have been gifted and talented pupils. Their responses give us insight into the way in which these pupils want to learn. Linda's findings will help to inform the way we work, particularly with regard to teaching and learning styles.

Suggestions from linguists and non-linguists in Year 12 for making languages more appealing at GCSE

Pupils would like to see:
- more grammar lower down the school (including English grammar);
- more emphasis on cultural aspects;
- less vocabulary cramming and more thorough learning and practice of vocabulary;
- books to read (not reading from textbooks);
- more pupil presentation in front of the class;
- more small group work;
- video – 'something to watch in class';
- more translation;
- more freedom to choose what they find interesting to work on;
- better equipment, e.g. headsets for listening;
- English used at times for explanation.

This list makes very interesting reading in the light of the gifted and talented initiative. Pupils identify a desire for more presentation opportunities, more extended reading and more group work. They are in fact requesting a shift away from teacher-centred lessons, towards pupil-centred activities. They also identify a desire for more culture and more grammar. I will deal with grammar, cultural aspects and materials in the next two sections.

It is interesting to note that the pupils identify different ways of working. They want to do more pupil presentation. They want to do more group work. They would like to have an element of choice in their work. These findings have major implications for teaching styles and tie in with suggestions I have made in Chapter 2:

- matching content to maturity levels;
- involving pupils in content planning;
- planning in spontaneous opinion-giving from Key Stage 3;
- using pictures;
- using video;
- adopting pre-listening and pre-reading routines.

All too often, MFL teachers feel guilty when they are not all-singing and all-dancing. Of course, there is a major role for teacher-centred input in our teaching, but there is also an imperative for our pupils to be **more** involved in **more** of the learning. They are telling us that they do not want to accumulate vocabulary and rush from topic to topic. They are asking for 'less vocabulary cramming and more thorough learning and practice of vocabulary'. This implies setting up tasks where pupils are required to transfer vocabulary to different contexts. Such tasks are engaging and motivating for gifted and talented pupils. Display can help here, but we also as teachers need to be aware of how we can do this from lesson to lesson. By following a grammatical overview and ensuring that structures are regularly recycled, we can help them to be confident about transferring language.

Linda Fisher's pupils have gone some way to defining the pedagogy we should employ:

> ... *a grammatically based communicative approach, where the learner is at the centre of the teaching and learning.*

The gifted and talented initiative is encouraging us to look at these issues and act on a day-to-day basis.

What about grammar?

As we have seen, pupils express the desire to learn more grammar earlier on. The National Literacy Strategy will help teachers in this regard, as pupils arrive with a clearer sense of structure and with more awareness of grammatical structure and grammatical terms. Language departments should be abreast of the strategy (**www.standards.dfes.gov.uk/literacy**) and in conversation with their English teaching colleagues to ensure effective delivery.

More able pupils often find grammar particularly liberating as it enables them to make connections, to analyse and identify patterns in order to subsequently apply them, thus affording them more creativity. This is surely one of the most rewarding aspects of teaching, when pupils take off and play with the structure of language. A cohesive approach to grammar will benefit all pupils, but will be especially valuable and motivating to the more able and will enable them to raise their game.

How to teach grammar constitutes a large book in itself. I offer some strategies that are based mainly on games, which worked for me and helped to demystify and activate grammar for all of my pupils, but were obviously of immense benefit for the more able.

A few starting points:

- Grammatical progression should be planned across the Key Stages. Topics can be usefully viewed as a vehicle for language structures, not as an end in themselves. The QCA format for the scheme of work, which allows for differentiation, showing extension activities with a diamond, is helpful.

  (See Appendix 1 for an example of a Key Stage 3 and a GCSE Spanish grammatical overview.)

- Grammar should be taught preferably in context, but this is not completely essential. Occasions may arise where a grammatical point is discussed in isolation because it has been raised by a pupil or by a teacher. Grammar points are planned into our schemes of work and may well be taught within a particular context, but if they are to be transferable, teachers must convey to the pupils the notion of re-usable structures and must demonstrate across contexts how these work. One of the main aims for catering to gifted and talented pupils, and indeed for raising standards across the board, should be to encourage transfer of grammatical structures across contexts. Similarly, where grammar points arise spontaneously, these opportunities should be exploited and grammar points should be discussed. There is also an argument for setting up grammatically-based games, which allow pupils to put rules into practice through activities embracing all four skills. The aim of these games should be to encourage transfer. Hence my contention that grammar should be taught in context where possible, but should then be obviously transferable.

- Grammar should be 'seen, heard, written and said'.

- Grammar should be discussed and explained, although not necessarily by the teacher. Pupils often find ways to explain that are infinitely more creative than the teacher's versions.

- Pupils should be allowed to express rules in their terms, as well as accepting our terms. It is important that a shared metalanguage is established. The National Literacy Strategy helps us with terms, but as Eric Hawkins points out: ' The simple principle to be followed throughout is to try to help pupils to conceptualise the *function* of each part of speech before seeking a *name* for it.' (Hawkins, 1984) In a classroom situation, we need to set up for gifted and talented pupils the opportunity to use and apply grammar, then the opportunity to analyse rules and further transform language. It is this 'insight into pattern' (Hawkins) that will move them forward. Pupils can teach each other and explain rules in their own terms, using their own examples and analogies. Such a shared approach to conceptualisation is often more successful than an imposed and little discussed metalanguage.

Beginnings and endings of lessons provide key moments for revision and recycling, for approaching grammar dynamically and revising grammar perhaps already covered in a creative way. It is a question of routine. We can usefully compare grammar teaching to our approach to the target language – if pupils come into our classrooms expecting to start with some grammar games, or a listening exercise with a grammatical element, or a speaking task based on a particular structure, they will soon accept and adopt that routine and the benefits will become apparent in their readiness to transfer language to new contexts.

Games/fun things to make grammar fun and stick

Grammar challenges pupils and it can also be fun. The centrality of an understanding of verbs and tenses to success in language learning is undisputed. We need to provide instances where pupils practise a range of verb forms as often as possible, where different learning styles are also catered for, so that pupils can see, manipulate, hear and produce utterances. The games I propose may not be 100% communicative in the purest sense of the term, but my aim is to provide a fun and challenging context for practice on the way to communication and expression.

Noughts and crosses

A classic, popular game which can be played in class teams or in pairs, in any tense, with any verb, or adapted to different tenses and different verbs, depending on the needs of the class.

ich	*du*	*er*
wir	*ihr*	*Sie*
man	*es*	*sie*

For example – *machen* – to do, practising the present tense:

- The teacher writes the infinitive on the board and divides the class into two teams – noughts and crosses.
- The noughts begin, looking to put their mark perhaps in the top right-hand corner. A pupil produces the correct form – *er macht* – and spells it out in German.

- The crosses decide to go for the middle square and spell out *ihr macht.*

And so the game continues ...

The verb can be regular or irregular, chosen by the teacher or the pupils, chosen as the verb of the week ... Alternatively, the names of tenses can figure in the boxes with a person and a verb – the possibilities are immense! Noughts and crosses can be as hard or as easy as we wish to make it.

Fun with dice

Similarly, verbs can be practised for short bursts during a lesson using dice. These dice can be ordinary dice, where the numbers correspond to a person:

1	*yo*	4	*nosotros*
2	*tu*	5	*vosotros*
3	*ella*	6	*ellos*

Or you can make your own dice using blank dice available from any Maths catalogue supplier!

As with noughts and crosses, fun with dice can be made challenging:

Throw 1 = verb	Throw 2 = person	Throw 3 = tense
1 *faire*	1 *je*	1 present
2 *venir*	2 *tu*	2 perfect
3 *avoir*	3 *il*	3 future
4 *prendre*	4 *on*	4 imperfect
5 *mettre*	5 *vous*	5 conditional
6 *être*	6 *elles*	6 immediate future

All examples need to be correctly pronounced and spelt out. There is an element of policing and you may need to think of a display that pupils can refer to if needs be, but the enjoyment is generally such that these are minor problems.

Emily Daly, who teaches in Cardiff, has produced some excellent 'Talking dice' which can be used from Year 7 to sixth form.

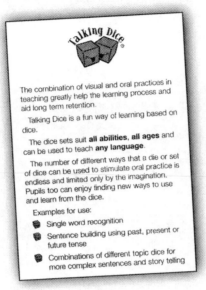

The combination of visual and oral practices in teaching greatly help the learning process and aid long term retention.

Talking Dice is a fun way of learning based on dice.

The dice sets suit **all abilities**, **all ages** and can be used to teach **any language**.

The number of different ways that a die or set of dice can be used to stimulate oral practice is endless and limited only by the imagination. Pupils too can enjoy finding new ways to use and learn from the dice.

Examples for use:

- Single word recognition
- Sentence building using past, present or future tense
- Combinations of different topic dice for more complex sentences and story telling

Dominoes

Gifted and talented pupils can be given grids and encouraged to make their own versions of dominoes for others to play. For example:

il avait	arrivé	il était	allé	il était	parti
elle avait	venu	elle était	discuté	il avait	repartie
elle était	voulu	il était	retourné	il avait	arrivée

The beauty of these games – apart from the fact that pupils enjoy playing them – is that they can reappear at any moment as a source of revision.

Battleships

Battleships is an excellent game for getting pupils to practise structure. Give the pupils the five sentences you want them to practise. You can invite contributions from the class here. Leave them to plot their sentences on their grids. Pupils then play the classic battleship game trying to sink each other. Gifted and talented pupils can be briefed to prepare the input if you wish.

For example – to practise making excuses, *müssen* and inversion in German:

Leider muss ich meine Hausaufgaben machen.
Leider muss ich meiner Mutter beim kochen helfen.
Leider muss ich meinen Großvater besuchen.
Leider muss ich einkaufen gehen.
Leider muss ich mein Zimmer aufräumen.

To be plotted on a grid:

	a	b	c	d	e
1					
2					
3					
4					
5					

An alternative version of this game is to provide the pupils with an outline as featured below and they simply mark their cross and then play. I find this more effective with the less able. In fact, the gifted and talented are able to invent their own sentences to play with.

	j'ai mangé	j'ai dessiné	j'ai vu	j'ai interviewé
une pomme				
un chat				
mon ami				
ma sœur				

Of course, an element of nonsense language – in my view humour – may arise. This is no bad thing. It goes without saying, however, that meaning needs to be firmly established. Pupils need to know what they're saying or what they want to say. Games are a way of allowing them more opportunities to have a go than they might otherwise get. The process of practising helps fix the structure in their minds.

Who wants to be a millionaire?

The format of this game works brilliantly in the classroom and pupils vie to make up their own questions. Of course the teacher gets to be Chris Tarrant, which is fun. This is a good game for involving the gifted and talented as it is useful for highlighting mistakes and raising grammatical awareness. At KS3, questions can be made up fairly simply. At a more advanced level, question planning is essential, but good fun and very rewarding.

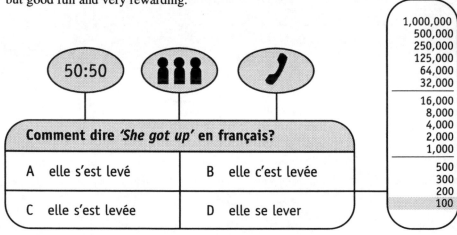

Board games

Board games are available to buy and figure in some coursebooks. In fact, pupils often come up with brilliant board games if provided with an empty grid and the structures to be practised. Board games are also a good source of spontaneous language. Gifted and talented pupils relish the creation of board games as an opportunity to put their creativity into practice. Here is an example of an AS level German game:

Ich vertrete die Ansicht ...	Mann kann nicht leugnen ...	Es kommt darauf an, ob ...	Ich muss zugeben ...

The death penalty should be reintroduced [1]	Maths and English should be compulsory in the sixth form [2]	Cars should be banned from inner cities [3]	**1**↓ [4]
GM foods should be banned [8]	Communism is the only fair political system [7]	← **2** [6]	Language learning is a waste of time for English speakers [5]
Marriage is an anachronism [9]	← **3** [10]	The popular press should respect privacy more [11]	You should be able to vote at 16 [12]
→ **4** [16]	Killing is never justified [15]	Abortion is murder [14]	Students should be paid to study [13]
Cannabis should be legalised [17]	TV causes violence [18]	← **5** [19]	I would like to live for ever [20]

Source: Colin Christie

Here, pupils must use the opinion-giving vocabulary provided in the top four boxes to offer points of view across topics depending on which squares they land on. The stimulus is in English, making the task more difficult. The large numbers work like ladders sending players forward or back, depending on the dice. The aim is obviously to get to the end of the board first.

Grammar auction

A grammar auction consists of providing groups of pupils with a finite sum of imaginary money, which they can use to purchase five grammatically correct sentences out of a possible ten sentences. Such an activity leads to much useful grammatical discussion and negotiation.

For example:

Pupils are given 300 Euros. They must bid for the correct sentences out of the following:

- *Je me suis levé hier à six heures du matin.*
- *Normalement, j'ai pris le petit-déj dans la cuisine.*
- *Je te coiffe et je te brosse les dents.*
- *Je me lève tous les jours à neuf heures.*
- *Normalement je prends le petit-déj dans la cuisine.*
- *J'ai l'habitude de regardé la télé le matin.*
- *Je me coiffe et je me brosse les dents.*
- *J'ai l'habitude de regarder la télé le matin.*
- *Je me suis lever hier àsept heures du matin.*
- *Je me leve tous les jours à neuf heures.*

This example is taken from a particular topic area and is focusing on tenses. There are also right and wrong possibilities. Grammar auction does not need to be so structured. It can be used as a good source of revision for both grammar and vocabulary and can be more or less difficult. Again, gifted and talented pupils can come up with the sentences to be bid for.

Blockbusters

Blockbusters can be used for nouns, but this game idea can also be used to practise structures:

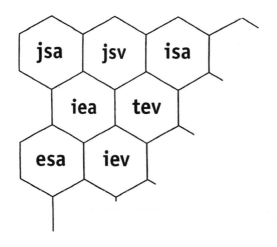

Pupils soon get used to saying *'je suis allé'*, *'je suis venu'*, *'il est allé'*. Of course, there is not a right or a wrong answer here and gifted and talented pupils will take the sentences wherever they wish them to go. Utterances can be extended by requiring a noun, an adverb, an expression of time.

Pictures can generate a whole sentence too:

He perdido mi bolsa – ¡qué lastima!

He perdido mi monedero – ¿qué voy a hacer?

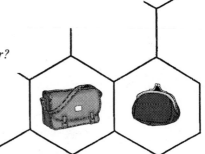

If pupils get into the routine of expecting to say more than the bare minimum, their productive skills will develop apace.

The four attainment targets

As well as adopting a grammar games routine, we can consider how effectively we use the four attainment targets to teach grammar. Gifted and talented pupils respond well to a variety of tasks. Spreading grammar across the AT ensures a rich diet.

AT1 – Listening is often used with an emphasis on answering, comprehending, ordering. As we have seen in Chapter 2, cognitively this is not necessarily very demanding. Why not use listening to highlight grammar? Transcripts are particularly useful in this respect.

AT2 – We can ask pupils to speak using five specific structures. We can help them give presentations by giving them skeleton outlines with grammatical content.

AT3 – As with listening, reading is ideal for grammar practice and for pattern identification. It lends itself well to using dictionaries to heighten language awareness.

AT4 – Grammar is not just about written accuracy. Nor is it about writing a rule which is then frequently disregarded. Again, grammatically based writing frames are useful (see p60) and use of reference material is also key.

Speaking, listening, reading and writing can all be set up with a grammatical focus as fairly independent, open-ended tasks for gifted and talented pupils.

Grammar and different learner styles

In order to help learners, we can consider different ways of recording grammatical rules.

- We can use shapes, colours, examples in context, which can then be displayed to remind pupils of a rule or structure.

- We can consider how grammar is recorded and we can involve our pupils in this process. Should they use books? Cards? Sticky notes? Do they tick off a rule when they have referred to it?

- We can use physical space to support grammatical awareness, having walls represent different genders and cases and using different signals for words which send the verb to the end.

It is useful to encourage pupils to put things into their own words. They may well see things differently. Visual learners respond well to physical displays and often come up with brilliant ways to present and display grammatical concepts. These may well help all pupils, not just our gifted and talented cohort.

Are our pupils stimulated by the materials we choose?

The reform of the National Curriculum and the GCSE examination has given us more freedom of choice in the subjects we approach. We can therefore consider how to widen both our horizons and those of our pupils. Our pupils want to know about culture. Do we adopt and impose a linguistic approach which is too simplistic? Do we concentrate too much on limited language content itself and not enough on cultural aspects?

We can consider:

- the range of materials we use. Linda Fisher's research highlights video as a welcome medium (see *InfoTech 4* (Hill 1999) which offers some very useful strategies for using video in language learning). We are now dealing with youngsters who are visually very sophisticated – TV and video games form a major part of their culture. We can aim to use these media on a regular basis, to re-inforce our classroom work or to consider cultural matters. Often a snippet is all that is needed. We can use generic worksheets such as the one that follows to exploit our clips. Again, it is a question of routine. Just as we can train pupils what to expect when dealing with pictures, the same can be achieved by using videos. The use of the word training does not stifle creativity. We can include meaningful tasks of a higher order for our gifted and talented learners, to exploit the material itself and our pupils' potential.

The breadth of the materials we use is also important. Gifted and talented pupils often respond well to resources designed to introduce more thought-provoking material to the languages classroom. *Allons en Haïti* is a pack produced by the charity Action Aid allowing pupils to 'investigate the lives of people in the Far West'.

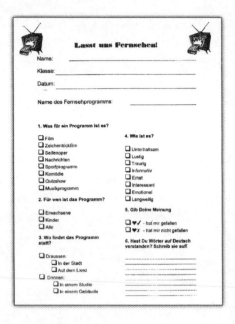

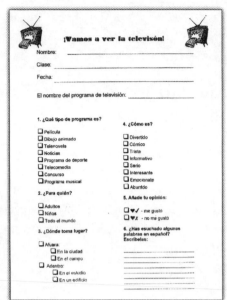

Generic satellite TV worksheet – source: Leanda Reed, Elliott School

MUNDI, the University of Nottingham's Centre for Development Education, produces resources in French about Mauritius and in German about Namibia. These are thought-provoking packs which will engage the curiosity of our most able pupils;

- using songs as a stimulus – modern songs or made-up songs, or songs which our pupils choose and actively want to understand. The following French website is useful in this respect **www.paroles.net**;

- cross-curricular projects or teaching through the medium of the language as a means of engaging gifted and talented pupils. Cross-curricular projects enable the more able to work with different content and to make links across subject lines. At The Grey Coat Hospital School in London, pupils studied Geography in Spanish in Year 9. At Hockerill Anglo-European School pupils study History and Geography through French at GCSE level. (See *'History and Geography through French: CLIL in a UK secondary school'* in Masih 1999.) Both projects are continuing. The problem as ever is one of accreditation. Examination boards do not offer a qualification that is examined through the medium of the foreign language. At the Anglo-European School, therefore, pupils study in the foreign language and are examined in English. Such a situation is obviously not ideal;

- contact with sixth-formers, mentors or native speakers, although we need to be even-handed here. As discussed in Chapter 1, FLA distribution should be treated with care.

How can we engage their interest?

Gifted and talented pupils want to read more. Again, this is a means of allowing them to follow their own interests and to direct their own learning. Extended reading is invaluable both for vocabulary acquisition and for learning strategies. At Elliott, we often carried out extended reading time in the library. Pupils were provided with a reading booklet, which acted as a record of their progress and their word discoveries. See the example on the next page. (See also Pathfinder 36: *More reading for pleasure in a foreign language* by Ann Swarbrick.)

There are many stimulating materials that all learners like to read. Of particular note are the *La loupe* readers published by Hodder and Stoughton, which deal with popstars, supermodels and gangsta rap and are incredibly motivating. CILT publishes an information sheet – number 33 – which details readers that are available.

As well as using readers, however, most pupils are more than happy to flick through *L'équipe* or the French, German or Spanish equivalents of *Hello* or *Heat*.

What about ICT?

ICT has the power to shift the focus from teacher to learner. The learner takes charge, developing his or her independence in language learning while the teacher plans and facilitates. Such an approach is attractive for many gifted and talented learners. ICT also permits easy access to different cultures and a wide range of resources, thereby affording us the opportunity to expand pupils' horizons and extend learning opportunities. ICT can therefore be viewed as a major tool in providing for the needs

INFORMATIONS

Titre:

Auteur:

Il s'agit de:

Je l'ai trouvé …

Ennuyeux	
Facile	
Mauvais	
Génial	
Assez intéressant	
Intéressant	
Très intéressant	
Difficile	
Superbe	
Touchant	

et aussi …

Lent	
Amusant	
Tragique	
Comique	
Romantique	
Realistique	
Intellectuel	
Passionnant	
Sensationel	
Nul	

et aussi …

POUR VOUS AIDER

FRANÇAIS	ANGLAIS
GENRE	
C'est …	It is …
un roman …	
d'aventure	an adventure story
d'espionnage	a spy story
d'amour	a love story
de guerre	a war story
de science fiction	a science fiction story
un policier	a police story
une bande dessinée	a cartoon
un livre de …	a book about …

PERSONNAGES

FRANÇAIS	ANGLAIS
Mon personnage favori s'appelle …	My favourite character is called …
Le personnage que je n'aime pas	The character I don't like
Il / Elle est …	He / She is …
agréable	pleasant
agressif (-ive)	aggressive
aimable	kind
amusant (-e)	fun
bête	stupid
courageux (-euse)	brave
drôle	funny
égoïste	selfish
fier (-e)	proud
honnête	honest
impatient (-e)	impatient
méchant (-e)	spiteful
paresseux (-euse)	lazy
sensible	sensitive
sérieux (-euse)	serious
sportif (-ive)	sporty
sympa	nice
timide	shy
il/elle a mauvais caractère	s/he is unpleasant

Reading booklet extract – source: Eleanor Mayes, Elliott School of gifted and talented pupils. All pupils, especially gifted and talented pupils can use technologies to research and to create language. As Bernardette Holmes points out, new technologies offer pupils the opportunity to 'drive the engine' in relation to grammar where they can present and exemplify grammatical points using contemporary contexts.

The National Curriculum mentions ICT in the following contexts:

Developing language skills

Pupils should be taught:

h techniques for skimming and scanning written texts for information, including those from ICT-based sources;

j how to redraft their writing to improve its accuracy and presentation including the use of ICT.

Developing cultural awareness

Pupils should be taught about different countries and cultures by:

a working with authentic materials in the target language including some from ICT-based sources ...

Breadth of study

During Key Stages 3 and 4, pupils should be taught knowledge, skills and understanding through:

d producing and responding to different types of spoken and written language, including texts produced using ICT.

e using a range of resources, including ICT, for accessing and communicating information.

If we succeed in including these suggestions within our teaching, our pupils' diet will indeed be enriched. Using ICT promotes independence and creativity also, depending on the task. Furthermore, many ICT activities can take place beyond school time. For gifted and talented pupils, creative use of ICT is often a liberating experience. They can sign up for an on-line course. They can explore challenging authentic resources. They can access culture and communicate with young people their own age.

The TTA provides some excellent exemplification materials for the use of ICT in MFL for all. These can be found at **www.canteach.gov.uk/itt/providers/ ICT_booklets/aamfl.doc**.

Creating Web pages

Our pupils' ICT skills may be well beyond our own. The creation of Web pages across topics is a wonderful way to engage gifted and talented pupils. Bernardette Holmes suggests joint website projects with partner schools.

Communicating with their peers in different cultural contexts

E-mail projects are becoming more and more popular. They are motivating for all, but particularly for gifted and talented pupils as they allow them to use real language and to talk about things that they wish to talk about. Schools can find partners on the Windows on the World website (**www.wotw.org.uk**) or, if they wish to work individually, can sign up for an e-pal – see below. Michael Evans and Linda Fisher from Homerton College, Cambridge, have undertaken an exciting project where pupils from France, Belgium, England and Senegal react in a bulletin board format to weekly topics. A photo or an article is posted on the site and pupils in the respective countries give their opinions in the language they are learning. A discussion ensues. For example, a photo of Eminem was posted and pupils wrote what their opinion of him and his lyrics was. Pupils are placed in small groups and go on-line at different times to read and react. The project has the beauty of being open-ended and personal. This project has also given rise to further informal e-mail conversations. It is co-ordinated by Michael and Linda. Contact **mje1000@ hermes.cam.uk** for further details.

Using the Internet for research

I include a generic worksheet for using the Internet which allows pupils to pursue their own interests. Gifted and talented pupils often have a burning desire to research fairly obscure topics. An open-ended worksheet like the one below affords them the opportunity to do this.

Using the Internet

The Internet allows us to exploit material that is right up to date and to access areas that are of real interest to the pupils:

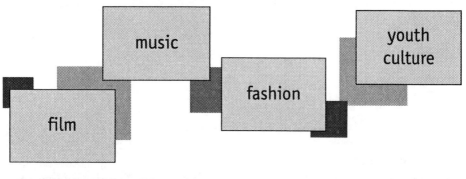

Website address:	
Contents:	
Five new words you found there with English meanings:	
Marks out of ten for this site:	
Who should visit it?:	

Homework possibilities: Teacher provides key word and search engine, pupils work to generic worksheet (see below).

Mapping their search: Teacher encourages pupils to show the route of their search so that they become more effective users.

Processing information: Information found can be edited and displayed in class to accompany the generic worksheet. Technologically-minded classes can establish the 'website of the week' slot.

News/magazine sites

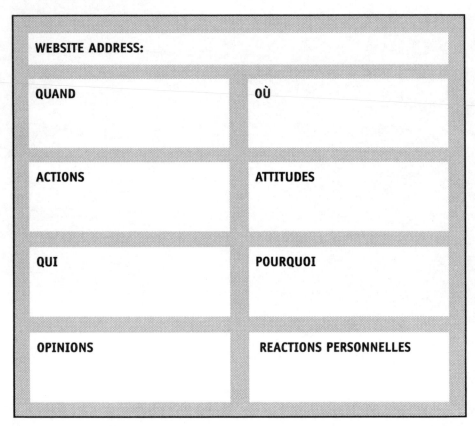

WEBSITE ADDRESS:	
QUAND	**OÙ**
ACTIONS	**ATTITUDES**
QUI	**POURQUOI**
OPINIONS	**REACTIONS PERSONNELLES**

The use of this worksheet can lead on to a cross-age news club run by sixth-formers or KS4 pupils. The editor defines the content and article length.

Such a project can be determined by pupils' interests, i.e. fashion, football, music, skateboarding, films.

- **www.xcalibre.ac.uk** The DfES is currently working in conjunction with the University of Cambridge to establish a website designed to identify resources and to share good practice in the education of gifted and talented pupils. The site offers ideas for pupils and teachers and encourages pupils to learn independently on the Web.

- **www.well.ac.uk** offers well documented links to online courses or grammatical exercises in a whole host of languages.

- **www.slf.ruhr-uni-bochum.de/email/idxeng00.html** allows pupils to find an e-partner with whom to learn in tandem.

- **http://Mikesradioworld.com** offers access to local radio sites around the world, ideal for independent listening.

Multimedia presentations

Pupils are often streets ahead of us so far as communicating information using ICT is concerned. PowerPoint is now recognised as a valuable teaching tool and we can encourage our pupils to present their work to the class using whichever ICT programmes our systems can support. Gifted and talented pupils are asking for more pupil presentation, let's give them the chance to do it. If you feel that this really isn't practical within a classroom situation, breakfast, lunchtime or twilight clubs – ideally run by sixth-formers or Year 10/11 pupils – can afford us the opportunity and the expertise to achieve the above.

Developing pupil autonomy

Bernardette Holmes suggests developing pupil autonomy through data processing and problem-solving simulations, locating appropriate Internet sites and setting up fields in a data processor to enable pupils to solve problems. Some may like to search the Web themselves and set their own challenges for their peers.

Suitable contexts could be:

- finding an appropriate apartment for an imaginary or real couple;
- furnishing a new house;
- booking a holiday for your own family or the Simpsons;
- planning an itinerary;
- booking a hotel and planning a honeymoon weekend for the stars of your choice.

key points	• Gifted and talented pupils want to do more of the learning
	• Gifted and talented pupils are often turned on by grammar
	• Beginnings and endings of lessons provide key moments for revision and recycling of grammar
	• Games created for or by gifted and talented pupils can be tremendously motivating
	• All four ATs can serve well to teach and practise grammar
	• Pupils respond well to different media

Enriching gifted and talented pupils' experiences – tailoring the curriculum offer to their needs

☐ Can our pupils see connections between languages and other subjects?

☐ What are the advantages of acceleration or fast-tracking?

☐ Are there any disadvantages?

☐ What are masterclasses?

☐ What about summer schools?

☐ What other enrichment opportunities could we develop?

☐ Are there any higher exams for our more able pupils?

chapter 5

Can our pupils see connections between languages and other subjects?

The study of languages brings the opportunity to examine one's own mother tongue in detail. We can also enrich the learning experiences of all pupils by making cross-curricular links, making links between subjects and areas of knowledge. Content and language integrated learning can be immensely stimulating and satisfying. Departments can work together at a very simple level to reinforce pupils' knowledge. For example, all MFL teachers in Year 7 at Elliott taught countries, rivers and mountain ranges when Geography was covering the same topic. The displays that we produced were beautiful and pupils felt that their knowledge was being reinforced and extended. Content and language integrated learning is particularly suitable for able pupils as it caters to their desire to make links and connections. It also circumvents the issue of 'having something to say'. While buying a litre of petrol is context-embedded and not very challenging, looking at Geography or History can both go on at an appropriate maturity level and provide a context which is intrinsically more challenging as it implies a body of knowledge rather than just a transaction.

Content and language integrated work can bring the 'content' which gifted and talented pupils often crave. Departments can include mini-topics within their schemes of work. It also does wonders for inter-departmental relationships. As mentioned in Chapter 4, Michael Ullmann from Hockerill Anglo-European School has written a very thought-provoking article on learning through the medium of the foreign language in *Learning through a foreign language – models, methods and outcomes* (ed Masih). He describes the curriculum implications, the pupils' perception, the model and the outcomes, although he does highlight the ongoing problem of accreditation. All pupils, however, were delighted at their progress in French.

Michael concludes:

> *To become and remain globally competitive, the British must start taking language learning seriously, go beyond communicative methodology and plan to take on the mantle of content and language integrated learning. We at Hockerill took that brave step a few years ago and there are no regrets. Now pupils and staff are applying in increasingly large numbers to sign up for bilingual education.* (p105)

Again, as mentioned in Chapter 4, The Grey Coat Hospital School teaches a Geography module in Spanish, while at Elliott School in Putney, gifted and talented pupils who took their GCSE language early in Year 9 subsequently studied History through French as part of their AS level course. The process challenges the more able, encouraging curiosity on their part, highlighting linguistic challenges via an age-appropriate, cognitively challenging content.

Science Across Europe is another project worth investigating – currently, nine units are available in ten languages. This project integrates language work and scientific content and focuses on the type of challenge which engages the gifted and talented pupil. (Contact Science Across Europe, The Association for Science Education, College Lane, Hertfordshire AL6 9AA.)

What are the advantages of acceleration or fast-tracking?

Some definitions are useful here. Acceleration means enabling pupils to progress at a faster rate than their year group through one or more subject areas (ReCAP), i.e. to work at an accelerated pace through the normal syllabus, while fast-tracking refers to any system for acceleration that enables pupils to take qualifications earlier than their year group. The DfES, however, holds fast-tracking to mean when groups of peers are promoted above their age peers. For the purposes of this book, the former definition will apply, where pupils are entered early for examinations.

There is much debate about the 14–19 exam system currently. The new AS level requires pupils to take exams three years in a row and the GCSE is currently under scrutiny as an exam in itself. The Specialist Schools initiative and Excellence in Cities have provided a structure and funds for experimentation in this domain and many Language Colleges have opted to fast-track their most able pupils towards GCSE, some at the end of Year 9, some at the end of Year 10. Results have been encouraging. Fast-tracking generally requires setting. The teacher is thereby able to pitch at a more specific level – of course, as with any set, differentiation still comes into play.

The advantages of fast-tracking include the following:

- Pupils can work at an accelerated pace in accordance with their ability.
- Pupils can attempt work which matches their maturity level.
- Pupils can aim for higher levels.
- Pupils can add an extra GCSE to their crop.
- Pupils can begin AS levels early, thereby adding an AS to their results.
- Teachers can plan challenging tasks into their teaching – tasks which involve comparing and contrasting, opinions and judgements, creativity and originality, synthesis and analysis.

After fast-tracking to GCSE, some Language Colleges have opted for the study of AS level over two years, whereas others have instituted an enrichment programme in L2, while introducing pupils to another foreign language L3. The case study at the end of this book considers the model of accelerated learning adopted by The Grey Coat Hospital School in London.

Are there any disadvantages?

What comes after the GCSE if it is taken early? In some ways, this is the most important question. Many schools are clamouring for exams such as History through French, Geography through French. Sadly, the market for these is too small. Given this situation, once the GCSE has been taken, which exams are suitable? Is the AS the best option? The question of maintaining momentum is also important. If pupils are studying an enrichment programme in KS4 or Year 11, do they lose momentum? Do they become demotivated or less focused because they are not studying specifically for an exam?

These are serious questions and the answers are only now appearing. The most common model would seem to be to work towards GCSE in Year 10, with an enrichment course running in Year 11 and the opportunity to do a second foreign language also. Enrichment courses offer real scope for creativity and originality. Topics far from the specifications can be chosen and pupils can work on cultural matters and pursue their own interests.

While undertaking AS level in Key Stage 4 is stimulating, rewarding and good for self-esteem, it may be at odds with timetabling possibilities. The study of AS early also often precludes the study of the second foreign language.

When fast-tracking is being considered, serious thought must be given to progression. Sensitive handling of the fast-tracked cohort is also essential. The decision to fast-track places provision for gifted and talented children high on the agenda. The group itself must be handled sensitively, the learners will need confidence and cosseting. The timetable must also permit movement between groupings in case of difficulty amongst some pupils. For fast-tracking to be successful, parents must be involved from the outset and staffing must be considered carefully.

Individuals can of course be fast-tracked. Here again, thought must be given to provision for the individual after the exam has been taken. Can he or she join an AS class? Will the timetable permit this? Can he or she work on a regular basis with the FLA, a PGCE student or a sixth-former?

Remarkably, some schools in Greenwich fast-track groups of children with excellent results without any timetabled provision. *Chapeau!*

What are masterclasses?

Again part of the Excellence in the Cities programme, masterclasses come in all shapes and sizes. They may consist of targeted revision classes, for example, GCSE A/A* revision classes across a family of schools. They may take the form of departments discussing what they teach best and arranging to teach grammatical structures/topics accordingly. They may take the form of a sixth-former delivering an oral presentation to a Year 11 class as an example of what needs to be done in the run-up to examinations.

The masterclasses run by Elliott School in Putney involved our six partner primary schools and focused on language learning strategies. Pupils were selected over a period of a month, using a basket of measures, oral and aural assessment and a language aptitude test. They then studied French, German and Japanese for a term each, culminating in a residential experience in France. (See Chapter 3 for the French and German overview.)

In short, masterclasses are developed according to a school's situation. The beauty of one-off masterclasses is that they raise the profile of a subject and often engage pupils' interest.

What about summer schools?

Now part of the Excellence in Cities programme, summer schools come in all shapes and sizes.

Summer School – Haydon School, 2000

Françoise Vidal at Haydon School, a Language College, piloted a Gifted and Talented summer school for ten days where twenty-eight pupils worked with two teachers, two sixth-formers and a French classroom assistant. The aim of the project was to equip the pupils to be able to function entirely in French during a day trip to Calais and to produce a PowerPoint presentation to describe their experiences. The focus of the summer school was on thinking skills and research. It involved much group work and independent study working on the design of vocabulary books. The pupils' reception was unequivocal, they all proclaimed it a 'brilliant' experience. The pupils were mostly in Year 6 and were then taught as an accelerated group in Year 7.

Françoise Vidal is now County Adviser for MFL in Hertfordshire.

Summer School – Sir Bernard Lovell School, 2001

Rosanna Raimato, Curriculum Director for International and Cultural Studies at Sir Bernard Lovell School, near Bristol, co-ordinated a ten-day summer school in conjunction with the school's expressive arts department, with the focus on Arts and Culture. Sir Bernard Lovell work with ten partner primary schools as part of their community brief and also as part of the CILT primary good practice project. Rosanna and her team established selection criteria for participation in the project and worked with their partner schools to draw up a list of forty able linguists across the partner schools in Year 6. Only twenty would attend the summer school, with the remaining pupils to be involved in similar enrichment days throughout the school year.

Pupils in Years 7 and 8 were chosen as mentors for the Year 6 pupils who had been selected to take part in the project, with a view to laying the foundation for the mentoring programme for gifted and talented pupils which the school runs as a matter of course. These Year 7 and 8 pupils worked alongside the Year 6 pupils for the duration of the summer school.

As many pupils had been studying French already, Rosanna and her team decided to begin the summer school with Japanese. Staffing consisted of Rosanna herself, the school's Japanese intern and one primary school teacher. Members of the expressive arts and ICT departments were also involved, but only attended on those days they were co-ordinating.

Sir Bernard Lovell worked with the Holburne Museum in Bath to set up a Japanese day where pupils considered Japanese artefacts and were involved in a printmaking session. Japanese language content was designed to allow pupils to show Japanese-speaking visitors round the museum. It consisted therefore of the following language:

- greetings and introductions
- directions
- talking about the content of the different rooms in the museum.

All this with a view to putting together a guide to the museum in Japanese. On the expressive arts side, the art teacher and Japanese intern worked together with the pupils to produce kites, concertina books and origami. All pupils' work was to form the basis of a parents' day and subsequent exhibition. The cross-curricular nature of the summer school was designed to appeal to the need for able pupils to make links and of course, being a summer school, its purpose was fun as well as challenging. Rosanna and her team were at pains to ensure that these pupils acquired skills that were new to them. The final day of the Japanese days was therefore led by an ICT specialist and devoted to the creation of webpages on the project.

The four remaining days were devoted to French. The first day consisted of a visit to Bristol with a guided tour of the town in French, the language focus being very much on structure:

- *il y a*
- *on peut voir*
- *voici*
- *plus loin*

An important part of the tour consisted of a visit to a large bookshop to purchase some English language children's books. The subsequent task for the pupils was to produce simplified professional-looking French versions of these books, which would form teaching materials for Sir Bernard Lovell and their partner primaries. Pupils used ICT to produce their versions, which were then laminated.

The last day saw an exhibition of work and a performance of Japanese and French role plays for teachers and parents. The turn-out was 100%.

Rosanna plans several follow-up days to pick up the remaining tranche of selected pupils, including an enrichment day to consider how Christmas is celebrated. The cross-curricular nature of this project, the element of independent work involved and the range of skills and tasks involved combine to make it an excellent example of how we can engage our gifted and talented pupils beyond the curriculum.

For more information, visit the Sir Bernard Lovell website at **www. sblonline.org.uk**.

Guidance for setting up summer schools can be found on the DfES standards site at **www.standards.dfes.gov.uk/studysupport**.

What other enrichment opportunities could we develop?

Gifted and Talented programmes operate within the curriculum and beyond the curriculum. Careful consideration of the timetable, adoption of independent working strategies, ensuring access to higher order tasks and a range of resources and reference materials provide the most tangible enrichment opportunities one can offer.

Extra-curricular activities are of immense value, however. Opportunities include the following:

- Taster courses or language festivals – gifted and talented pupils can be involved in the organisation of these, can be taught and can even teach! One model is to work with one's family of schools, to survey the languages offered by staff and by pupils and to identify those less commonly taught. A target year is decided upon and the number of gifted and talented pupils per school defined. The day then works as a carousel of fun activities.

- Breakfast clubs – with the problem of fitting subjects on the timetable, breakfast clubs are becoming increasingly popular both for homework support and also for development opportunitities for new languages. For example, breakfast Italian is carried out very successfully at Gosforth High School.

- University access programmes – some schools run university access programmes, which include visits to universities and university summer schools, but also in-school lectures pitched at a higher level designed to help pupils make an informed choice regarding their studies at university. Language professionals are often invited in to contribute to the programmes.

- Revision masterclasses within one's family of schools – these are often set up at GCSE level and targeted at A/A* pupils, working particularly on extending utterances and improving grammatical accuracy.

- International newspaper day – where pupils work on combining ICT languages and extended writing to produce an international newspaper. Older pupils who mentor gifted and talented pupils can co-ordinate or help to run such events. Pupils work collaboratively and to deadlines to produce a finished product.

- Lunchtime clubs/Twilight sessions for new languages – the curriculum is overloaded, yet many gifted and talented pupils jump at the chance of learning a new (often third) language after school. Italian, Spanish, Japanese, Portuguese can be introduced in this way if people are willing to be flexible about time.

- Saturday schools can come in all shapes and sizes. Funding is available for Saturday school provision. Go to **www.standards.dfes.gov.uk.excellence/ policies/GiftedAndTalented**.

- E-projects – as outlined in Chapter 4, these can be motivating for pupils as they involve writing for a real audience, authentic reading tasks and also a broadening of cultural horizons.

- Intensive days – at Elliott, PGCE students from Roehampton Institute worked with class teachers on a grammatically-based intensive French day, where pupils went from group to group practising different structures in different contexts. In Leeds, the Comenius Centre hosted a French day for four Wakefield schools as part of the Wakefield Area Schools Project (WASP) involving Queen Elizabeth Grammar School, Ossett School, Wakefield Girls' High School and The Cathedral School. The aim of the day was to encourage the pupils to speak French and to expose them to some new activities and ways of learning. It was made up of a series of four sessions that all pupils attended at some point during the day and the focus was on imagination and creativity. Here is an example of one of the poems produced during the day of activities:

Le bonheur

Le bonheur est blanc

Le bonheur a le goût de cannelle

Le bonheur sent comme un forêt

Le bonheur fait penser à la pluie

Le bonheur ressemble au lever du soleil

Le bonheur a la sensation du poil de chat

Le bonheur fait penser aux montagnes en Autriche

J'aime le bonheur

Jazmyn Henderson

More details on the project can be found at **www.tasc.ac.uk/depart/comenius/index.htm**.

- Displays – intensive days, lunchtime clubs, festivals, competitions … All of the enrichment opportunities mentioned here can form the basis of meaningful displays. Gifted and talented pupils respond well to themed displays.

- School journeys are invaluable for pupils. They allow them first-hand access to different cultures, thus enabling pupils to broaden their horizons. School journeys increasingly have a cross-curricular focus or project attached, or may include an element of work experience. Homestays or exchanges provide an excellent means of language practice and cultural insight. (See Pathfinder 30: *Crossing frontiers.*)

- European projects – Lingua or Comenius activities shift the focus of language lessons, thereby providing a welcome change for gifted and talented pupils. Details can be obtained by visiting the website of the Education and Training group of the British Council.

- Competitions – some of the major publishers run writing competitions which provide an excellent focus for all pupils, but particularly gifted and talented pupils, as the themes are often creative and provide learners with a real audience for their work. European competitions such as the European Awards for Languages also motivate gifted and talented pupils as well as raising the profile of languages. **www.cilt.org.uk/projects** posts details of the European Awards.

Are there any higher exams for our more able pupils?

Post–16, Advanced Extension Awards are to be available in French, German and Spanish. They replace special papers and have been trialled extensively. AEAs are aimed at the most able A level pupils and are really designed for A grade candidates. No teaching is required – most pupils simply turn up and sit the exam. The exam consists of:

Linguistic tests	15%
Reading comprehension	15%
Transfer of meaning into English	10%
Listening comprehension	10%
Extended writing	50%

The grading of the papers is Distinction, Merit, Unclassified.

key points	• Cross-curricular projects are an excellent way to motivate gifted and talented pupils
	• Masterclasses and summer schools come in all shapes and sizes
	• With flexible timetabling, many enrichment activities can be provided beyond the school day
	• Families of schools can co-operate to provide exciting experiences for the gifted and talented cohorts

Case Study: Accelerated Learning at The Grey Coat Hospital School, London

Our case study focuses on the Accelerated Learning project undertaken by Siân Maddrell, Head of Languages at The Grey Coat Hospital School, 1995–2000.

The Grey Coat Hospital School is a voluntary aided Church of England comprehensive school with 1000 pupils. The school is single sex – girls – in Years 7–11 with a mixed sixth form.

The languages department under Siân's leadership was interested in fast-tracking and also in Acclerated Learning theories. They decided therefore to embark on an experiment.

Accelerated Learning proceeds from the assumption that 'great minds don't think alike'. At The Grey Coat Hospital School, Siân and her team encouraged pupils in their top sets to identify their preferred learning style and their particular intelligence type:

- linguistic;
- mathematical and logical;
- visual and spatial;
- musical;
- interpersonal;
- intrapersonal;
- kinaesthetic.

Accelerated Learning is based on the premise that, since we all have different preferred ways of learning, a variety of approaches is important. There is music as background to the tapes, pictures to prompt words and expressions, role plays to act out, word games, relaxation exercises at the beginning of each act, English and TL, pupils are encouraged to highlight all present tenses in one colour, all perfect tenses in another, etc.

Pupils were made aware of different techniques for learning and were encouraged to examine **how** they were learning.

They were also encouraged to take ownership of their learning, their understanding, their confidence, their progress, their areas of weakness, etc.

Pupils also considered the implications of the learning pyramid for their methodology.

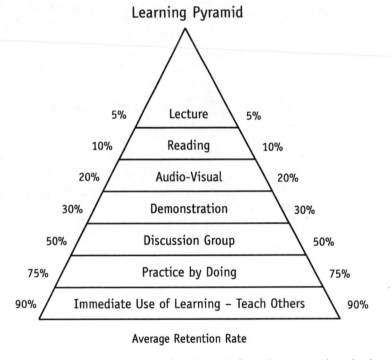

Learning Pyramid

5%	Lecture	5%
10%	Reading	10%
20%	Audio-Visual	20%
30%	Demonstration	30%
50%	Discussion Group	50%
75%	Practice by Doing	75%
90%	Immediate Use of Learning – Teach Others	90%

Average Retention Rate

Source: Accelerated Learning Systems Ltd

This diagram shows the best methods of retaining information. Note that the best four methods are related to actual repetition of the material 'learnt'. Use other people to test your RETENTION abilities. PARENTS, FRIENDS and FORM TUTORS can be recruited to help in this process. Show them what you know and perhaps you will teach them at the same time.

In languages, the theory of Accelerated Learning propounds an individual approach to learning skills and proposes that pupils must take ownership of their learner type. Learners must understand whether they learn via:

- visual stimulation – posters, videos, mind maps;
- auditory stimulation – listening to speakers, taking part in debates, responding to music;
- kinaesthetic stimulation – designing and building, 'showing';
- written stimulation – the written word.

There are six stages of learning for the Accelerated programme:

✔ state of mind

✔ information intake

✔ exploring the subject

✔ memorising information

✔ showing you know

✔ reflecting on what you learn.

In 1996, preparatory work for Accelerated Learning began. In service training took place, schemes of work were written and Accelerated Learning for all groups was introduced in French in Year 7. Lengthy discussion took place regarding the target groups for early entry to GCSE. The top two parallel gifted and talented French sets in Year 8 were to be the target groups.

In 1996, Italian Accelerated Learning was introduced for Year 12 students. This group studied GCSE Italian in one year – it was partly on the basis of the success of this group (taught by Flavia Lambert, who played a key role in the whole project) that The Grey Coat Hospital School decided to introduce Accelerated Learning in Year 7.

The Italian group has run every year since its introduction back in 1996 (even now with AS) and results are always excellent.

In 1999, the French cohort sat their GCSE examination in Year 9. The programme continued through subsequent years, with a second cohort sitting their Spanish GCSE exam in 2000 and a third cohort sitting their French exam in 2001. Meanwhile, the first cohort went on to study AS level French at Key Stage 4.

In Year 7, pupils were in mixed ability groupings and were placed in sets according to their ability in Years 8 and 9. Time allocation was as follows:

Year 7 – 3 x 45 minute lessons per week
Year 8 – 3 x 45 minute lessons per week
Year 9 – 4 x 45 minute lessons per week

Accelerated Learning materials are based on a narrative and place a great deal of emphasis on the story. Indeed, the English is given next to the French. Listening plays a great part in the input of the story, each pupil has an individual cassette and there is a fair degree of independent learning. Listening is for **learning** rather than for testing. Listening also contributes to oral confidence as the pupils are encouraged to learn sections off by heart – they always know what every part of the section means and so can transfer their knowledge to other contexts more easily.

Vocabulary acquisition is clearly structured and results in oral confidence being gained fairly rapidly. The pattern of lessons is determined by the materials themselves although Grey Coat teachers felt the requirement to supplement the course with extra grammar and reinforcement exercises, particularly with focused written tasks in order to build up to effective coursework writing for GCSE.

Teachers were also at pains to make the links between the content and GCSE tasks explicit (the course is designed for adults, not specifically for the GCSE examination).

Disadvantages of Accelerated Learning

Siân and her team felt that the major disadvantages of Accelerated Learning were as follows:

- the cost;
- the fact that the course was intended for adults;

- the fact that certain GCSE topics therefore did not figure;
- the style of the pictures – although the youngsters didn't seem to mind;
- the pace of the cassettes – the pace of the cassettes is very good for learning but needs supplementing for the GCSE as GCSE tapes are faster;
- school time is not necessarily best suited to the relaxing element of AL techniques.

The results, however, speak for themselves:

Year 9 French GCSE results 1999

Group	A*	A	B	C	D	Total entries	% A*–A	% A*–C	% A*–G
X	4	15	5	1	-	25	76	100	100
Y	5	6	12	3	1	27	41	96	100
Total	9	21	17	4	1	52	59	98	100

Pupil reaction was overwhelmingly favourable:

Everyone rose to the challenge.

Helen

I feel that it was very beneficial to take it early. I don't feel that I will get a lower grade for taking it early.

Jennie

If I was ready to take my GCSE, why wait two years?

Nadya

I would like to thank my teacher for giving me such an excellent opportunity.

Asmara

I think having the sentences translated into English was really good.

Hollie

> The tapes are good as you can hear how to say the words as well as spell them.

> I think the Accelerated Learning scheme is excellent as you pick up information as the story progresses; it's like reading a novel, but you learn from it instead.

Emma

Veronica

The pupils' comments point up some gifted and talented favoured learning styles – sound–spelling relationship, the need for clarity and the desire for English translation to understand exactly how sentences break down, the desire to undertake more extensive reading.

All pupils felt a sense of achievement and have gone on to achieve well at AS level. The introduction of the scheme has also resulted in more dual linguists. The project led to two groups of 28–30 dual linguists in the first year.

Gifted and talented pupils have benefited enormously from the experience. As a consequence, other departments are now reviewing the fast-tracking option.

Siân Maddrell now teaches at Acland Burghley School in North London.

The Grey Coat Hospital School experiment achieved excellent outcomes and very high levels of motivation among able pupils. Subsequent AS level results were most pleasing. While the Accelerated Learning course is designed principally for adults, it is evident that the methodology appealed greatly to more able pupils, particularly the translation element and the grammatical input. This provides us with a useful conclusion for this book and for language teaching in general, namely that there can be no hard and fast exclusive methodology for gifted and talented pupils or indeed for any pupils. Different circumstances and different pupils require different approaches. There is no magical formula for teaching gifted and talented pupils: there are principles, which should inform our teaching. Pragmatism is the name of the game.

References

Adams, J. (2000). *French writing frames: creative and imaginative writing.* Folens.

Adams, J. with Panter, S. A. (2001). Pathfinder 40: *Just write!* CILT.

Buckland, D. and Short, M. (1993). Pathfinder 20: *Nightshift: ideas and strategies for homework.* CILT.

Convery, A. and Coyle, D. (1999). Pathfinder 37: *Differentiation and individual learners: a guide to classroom practice.* CILT.

Cummins, J. (1995) 'Differentiation and individual learners'. In: Hall, D. *Assessing the needs of bilingual pupils.* David Fulton Publishers.

Coyle, D. (1999). 'Supporting students in CLIL contexts'. In: Masih, J. (ed) *Learning through a foreign language: models, methods and outcomes.* CILT.

Harris, V. (1997). Pathfinder 31: *Teaching learners how to learn: strategy training in the Modern Languages classroom.* CILT.

Hawkins, E. (1984). *Awareness of language.* Cambridge University Press.

Hill, B. (1999). InfoTech 4: *Video in language learning.* CILT.

Laycock, J., Leyden, S. R. and Wallace, B. (1997). In: Teare, B. *Effective provision for able and talented children.* Network Educational Press Ltd.

McLachlan, A. (2001). *Métro 4.* Heinemann.

McNab, R. (1999). *Métro 1.* Heinemann.

Masih, J. (ed) (1999). *Learning through a foreign language: models, methods and outcomes.* CILT.

Snow, D and Byram, M. (1997). Pathfinder 30: *Crossing frontiers: the school study visit abroad.* CILT.

Swarbrick, A. (1998). Pathfinder 36: *More reading for pleasure in a foreign language.* CILT.

Useful addresses

MLG Publishing Ltd (Mini-Flashcard Language Games)
PO Box 1526
London
W7 1ND
Tel: 020 8567 1076
Fax: 020 8566 3930

Talking Dice
78 Brynteg
Cardiff
CF14 6TU
Tel: 029 2065 7364
E-mail: talkingdice@yahoo.co.uk
Website: www.talkingdice.co.uk

Accelerated Learning Systems Ltd
50 Aylesbury Road
Aston Clinton
Aylesbury
Bucks
HP22 5AH
Tel: 01296 631 177
Fax: 01296 631 074

Appendix 1

Elliot School: Key Stage 3 Scheme of Work – Spanish

Yr	U	Unit title	Unit contents	Grammar	Resources
7	1	*¡Hola!*	• simple questions • numbers 1–31 • alphabet • name, age, birthday • months, dates, days • classroom objects • classroom instructions	• verbs in 1st/2nd person sing. • indefinite articles • *hay/no hay* • plurals of nouns	*¡Arriba! 1, tema 1*
7	2	*La familia y los amigos*	• description of family, friends and pets – physical • nationalities • numbers 1–100 • Christmas, *fiestas*	• 3rd person sing. • all persons of regular *–ar* and *–ir* verbs • agreement of adjectives • intensifiers (*muy, bastante*) • definite article • *tener/ser* persent tense • possessive adjectives	*¡Arriba! 1 tema 3 pp38–47* *¡Arriba! 2 tema 2 pp36–37*

Yr	U	Unit title	Unit contents	Grammar	Resources
7	3	*El horario*	• school subjects and timetable • telling the time • mealtimes and simple items of food and drink	• *me gusta* • radical changing verbs – *preferir* and *pensar* • adverbs (*normalmente* etc) • regular –*er* verbs • irregular verb hacer	*¡Arriba! 1, tema 2*
7	4	*En casa*	• daily routine • simple descriptions of homes • describe a room • numbers above 100 • ordinal numbers (1st, etc)	• reflexive verbs • to be *ser* and *estar* • prepositions	*¡Arriba! 1, tema 3* pp48–54 *¡Arriba! 2, tema 1*
7	5	*En el pueblo*	• places in a town • points of compass and maps • following and giving directions • seasons • weather	• irregular verb –*ir* • positive imperative form of reg. verbs 2nd/3rd pers. sing.	*¡Arriba! 2, tema 1* pp18–19 *tema 4* pp58–59 pp66–73
7	6	*Pasatiempos*	• leisure, hobbies sport, music • family activities	• *gustar, preferir* + infinitive • present continuous • modal verbs *poder, querer* • interjections • subject pronouns *él, ella, usted* • *ir a* + infinitive	*¡Arriba! 1, tema 4* *¡Arriba! 3, tema 1* pp12–13

Yr	U	Unit title:	Unit contents:	Grammar:	Resources:
8	7	*Nos presentamos*	• character descriptions • meeting people formally and informally • being and welcoming a guest • expressing thanks in speech and in a simple informal letter	• qualifier *poco* • regular comparative and superlative adj. • formation of adverbs with *-mente* • direct object pronous (*le, la, les, las*)	*¡Arriba! 3, tema 2* pp38–39 *¡Arriba! 2, tema 4,* pp60–61 *¡Arriba! 2, tema 3* pp40–41
8	8	*La comida*	• food and drink • likes, dislikes and preferences • following and preparing recipes • buying food • restaurant/*tapas* • Christmas food	• direct object pronouns with thinks (*lo, la, los, las*) • expressions of quantity • *tener hambre/sed* • disjunctive pronoun with preposition *para mi*	*¡Arriba! 1, tema 5* *¡Arriba! 2, tema 2* pp24–31
8	9	*La salud*	• parts of the body • ailments, illness • visiting doctor/dentist • healthy lifestyle	• structure with *doler* • expressions with *tener* • structures using *deber, hay que, tener que* + infinitive	*¡Arriba! 1, tema 5* pp82–83, pp86–89 *¡Arriba! 4, tema 3* pp64–65

Yr	U	Unit title	Unit contents	Grammar	Resources
8	10	*De compras*	• shopping for clothes/presents • discussion of fashions • considering appropriateness of clothes	• expressions of size • demonstrative adj. and pronouns • use of interrogatives	*¡Arriba! 1, tema 6*
8	11	*El turismo*	• holidays and tourism • outings and trips • modes of transport	• preterite tense of *ir* • preterite tense of regular *–ar* verbs	*¡Arriba! 2, tema 5*
8	12	*Diversiones*	• entertainment • concerts, cinema theatre, sport, a bullfight • ordering and buying tickets • recounting a past event or outing	• all forms of preterite of *–er* and *–ir* reg. verbs • preterite of *hacer, ver, estar* • imperfect (receptive use) using *había/ hacía/era*	*¡Arriba! 2, tema 1, pp12–13* *¡Arriba! 3, tema 2, pp24–35*
9	13	*Nosotros los jóvenes*	• friendships • descriptions of people • jobs in the home • pocket money • telephoning • conveying messages • invitations	• relative pronoun *lo que* • giving and justifying opinions • expressions for apologising, accepting, thanking, excusing, telephoning	*¡Arriba! 3, tema 2 pp40–41* *¡Arriba! 3, tema 2 pp36–37* *¡Arriba 3!, pp56–57* *¡Arriba 2!, tema 1 pp10–11 pp14–15*

Yr	U	Unit title	Unit contents	Grammar	Resources
9	14	*Los medios de comunicación*	• different media (TV, newspapers, advertising, film) • understanding reviews • reading for pleasure	• irregular comparatives and superlatives • *tan* + adjective + *com/tanto/como* • suffix *–isimo* • imperfect tense	*¡Arriba! 3, tema 4* pp78–79
9	15	*Nuestros proyectos*	• future plans • options, choices • form-filling • writing a formal letter • jobs	• future tense • *ser* and *estar*	*¡Arriba! 3 tema 4*
9	16	*Nuestro medio ambiente*	• aspects of the environment • the future world	• negatives other than *no* • more work on commands	
9	17	*El mundo hispano*	• focus on one or more Spanish-speaking countries other than Spain	• writing a factual report • more complex written language	Internet *¡Arriba! 2, tema 6*
9	18	*¿Tú, qué opinas?*	• understanding and producing critical reviews	• relative pronoun *que* and subordination	

Unit	Core	Midrange	Extension
School	Imperative *tú/vosotros* form Indefinite article Definite article Possessive article Adjectives Numbers	Imperative reflexive form Present tense + *desde hace* Comparative *Si* + present tense Impersonal verbs – *hay que*	Pronouns Superlative Transative – *tomé el autobús*
Food Shopping	*De* after a quantity (*un kilo de …*) Negative *nunca* Subjunctive *quisiera*	Indefinite pronouns Pronouns *la, lo, los, las* Negative *ni … ni*	Demonstrative pronouns (*éste, ésta*) Negative infinitive
Myself, Family and Friends	Adjectives – agreement + use of *grande, pequeño, joven, viejo, bonito, guapo + gordo* before noun Present *ser, estar, tener* Reflexive *llamarse*	Imperfect *era, estaba, tenía, iba* Reflexive *entenderse, discutir* *Poder, querer* Perfect tense	Imperfect *estar, ser, tener* Pronouns *me entiende*
Clothes Shopping	Adjectives Negative *nunca*	Negative *ningún* Perfect tense	Pronouns *le, la, les, lo, los, las* Demonstrative pronouns (*éste, ésta*) Demonstrative adjectives
Free Time and Social Activities	Possessive adjectives Irregular verbs – *jugar, ir, salir, hacer* Present tense –*ar* verbs (*practicar*) Definite article	Imperfect tense Perfect tense Pronouns *me, te*	Negative *ningún* Prepositions *jugar a, ir a, salir con* Imperative 1st person plural
Life at Home	*Tener que* + infinitive *Hacer* present tense Reflexive verbs present tense		Possessive pronouns Reflexive verbs perfect tense
Home Town and Local Area	Definite article Imperatives *tú/vosotros* form	Comparatives	Comparative with *mejor*

Topic			
Home Town and Local Area (cont'd)	Adverbs – *muy, poco, mucho, demasiado, bastante*		
Health and Fitness	*Dolerse* Present tense + *desde hace* Imperative *tú/vosotros* form Reflexive verbs present tense Impersonal verb *hay que*	Impersonal verbs *se debe, me falta, se puede* *Antes de .../después de ...*	Reflexive verbs perfect tense Passive perfect tense
Further Education and Career	Conditional *me gustaría* Imperfect tense *era* Immediate future Omission of article before jobs	Conditional *sería, no podría* *Si* + present tense Perfect tense	*Cuando* + future tense *Si* + subjunctive Imperfect tense Future tense
L and C at Work			Present subjunctive
Travel at Home and Abroad	Present tense Perfect tense Imperfect tense *hacía, había, era* Immediate future *ir + a* Possessive adjectives Adjectives	Future tense Imperfect tense *Venir de* *Poder* + infinitive	Conditional tense *Si* + sequence of tenses (subjunctive) Negative ... *sólo*
Food and Drink	Definite article *De* + quantity Conditional *me gustaría*	Negative *ya no ...*	Pronouns Impersonal verb *hay que* Relative pronoun *que* Infinitive as imperative
Environment and Society	*Se puede* + infinitive Impersonal verb *hay que* Imperative *tú/vosotros* form Impersonal verbs *hace, hay* Immediate future (*ir + a*)	Future tense *tener, estar, ser* *Si* + present tense	Passive perfect tense Future tense
World Events and Issues	Adverbs of time and place	Use of infinitive after prepositions (*a/para/con*) *ir*	Perfect tense passive Relative pronouns *quien, que*

Appendix 2

What to look out for when identifying gifted and talented pupils

☐ Does he or she have excellent powers of retention and recall?

☐ Does he or she respond swiftly and confidently to extended listening passages?

☐ Does he or she have fun with language, making things up and transferring with ease from context to context?

☐ Does he or she respond well to grammar, wanting to know why, going beyond the classroom diet?

☐ Does he or she stay behind to discuss points further?

☐ Does he or she complete repetitive tasks quickly, often dismissing their importance?

☐ Is he or she easily bored during oral repetition?

☐ Does he or she want to write things down?

☐ Does he or she possess strategies for dealing with extended reading passages?

☐ Does he or she seek connections between English and the MFL?